Beautiful Thoughts

Judy Johnson

Hey David
thinking of you with
love Judy
xo

Judy Johnson 2019

Free to use at will

ISBN: 9781977530240

DEDICATION

To the ONE ~ Ocean of Knowledge.

May these drops reveal Your beauty.

iv

ACKNOWLEDGMENTS

*Thank you to those who have read and
supported the Daily Thoughts for years.*

*Your enthusiasm continues
to inspire their creation.*

*A special thank you to Carol MacLennan & Teri
Crawford for love and care in editing,*

*Anne-Marie McElrone for co-mothering
the Daily Thoughts,*

*the Halifax BK students who are masters of
'catching' a Daily Thought in morning class,*

and

Judi Rich for the beautiful cover.

DEAR READER

These thoughts are for you
who seek to be the best you can be
to support the best in humanity.

You may wish to keep the book by your
bedside to read before sleeping or use to
start your day.

You might use it as a guide for your daily
meditation practice, or as a companion kept
close during the day to read when you need
a lift or a re-direct.

For maximum benefit, take the time to
digest and contemplate each thought ~ one
per day.

These thoughts were inspired by the
spiritual knowledge of Raja Yoga as taught
by the Brahma Kumaris.

Their teachings are free of charge and their
meditation centres can be found at

www.brahmakumaris.org

WHY Beautiful Thoughts?

Thoughts can lift me up or bring me down.

Thoughts are an expression of my life energy.

Every thought creates a world inside my mind.

This world is expressed through my eyes, in my words and through my actions.

My outside world is shaped by my inside world.

Every creation begins with a thought.

To create a beautiful world, we need an endless stream of beautiful thoughts.

These thoughts are an attempt to distill the profound wisdom of Raja Yoga and make it accessible for practical use in daily living.

JANUARY

1

My world is a reflection of my inner state. When rushed and frenzied inside, my external world seems to move faster. When I move more slowly, the world slows in response. This is a practical expression of the relativity of time. Today let me use this understanding and move slowly to create a world of peace around me.

2

Collect moments of peace. When I take a deep breath, hold it for a quiet moment and offer a sweet smile to myself, I bring a drop of peace to my world. Each precious moment of peace adds a drop to the pond. Drop by drop, a pond becomes a lake, then an ocean of peace for the world. Today let me add a drop of peace to my world.

3

Do not take sorrow. When I say that someone has hurt me, I really mean that I took sorrow from the other person. It is up to me whether I allow someone's words or bad intentions to enter my inner world and affect me. If I take sorrow, I become hurt, angry and resentful. If someone tries to give me sorrow I can choose NOT to take it. Today I will not take sorrow.

4

Feelings freeze, hearts harden and minds muddle when senseless and confusing events happen in the world. Creating a place of warmth and comfort becomes an act of service at such a time. Keeping my inner fire lit, my vision pure and my feelings loving is the spiritual practice required during such times. Today let me be a place of warmth and comfort in a cold world.

5

A bad day is good data about what makes me react, where my sensitivities lie, how I respond when triggered and what leads me to take sorrow from others. Data, when well-interpreted, becomes knowledge. When I use this knowledge to adjust my thinking and my response to external triggers, I develop wisdom. Today let me use the data of a bad day to become wise.

6

A deep thinker will probe beneath the words and listen behind the sound to 'catch' meaning. When I don't understand something, I use my intellect to analyze the problem in search of clarity. This can become intellectual or over-analytical. A deep thinker, on the other hand, will sit quietly and invite insight to reveal a solution. Today let me 'see' meaning and solutions by thinking deeply.

7

In Greek, the word for meditation comes from the root word for dialogue. Meditation is having a sweet dialogue with my true self and with God. For this I must focus my attention to discern my subtle spiritual self, then reach my mind upwards to forge a connection to the Divine. This sweet dialogue is called meditation. Today let me enter a dialogue with myself and with God.

8

Black and white thinking is an expression of concrete-mindedness. This means seeing only the solid or physical aspects of a situation. This type of thinking is considered 'realistic' because it deals with the limits and constraints involved. However, possibilities exist in the space between black and white, where dreams reveal the full spectrum of our gifts and potential. Today let me think in technicolour and expand my sense of what's possible.

9

Imagine the mind as a library. Stored in the soul is a memory of everything I have ever experienced. Although I cannot remember the details, these experiences shape my perceptions and experience of living. In quiet moments, I can browse the bookshelves of my life and discover the wisdom I have accumulated. Today let me listen in silence and appreciate the wisdom I have stored within me.

10

Linkage or leakage? I accumulate inner power when my thinking is linked to elevated ideas and attuned to see the positive qualities in others. Power drains away when I let my thinking sink and I begin to see the weaknesses in others. Each day, I am either accumulating or leaking spiritual power. As a result, at the end of the day I feel refreshed or drained. Today let me choose to accumulate power by linking my thoughts to positive energy.

11

The greatest authority is the authority of experience. I may know many things, but until I have experienced them directly they remain theoretical. My wealth of experience becomes practical wisdom when I spend time in silent reflection. Solitude provides the incubator for discovery and wisdom. Today let me draw value from my experiences in solitude and enjoy the authority of my own experience.

12

The soul needs newness on a regular basis. The consistency of a healthy routine keeps me grounded and stable. However, without newness, it can become rote and boring. When bored, I look outside to change my situation, my clothes, my partner or my life. To generate newness, from the inside-out, I must stretch my intellect to create something interesting. Even the smallest innovation, when created myself, generates enthusiasm and motivation. Today let me stretch myself to create something new.

13

'Letting go' is the power to walk away from situations that hold me captive. Bad habits get me into limiting situations, which can feel like a cage. Over time, even a cage can become a comfort zone as I adjust myself and learn to cope. It requires courage to leave a comfort zone that I have called home for so long. Today let me free my mind and heart from cages.

14

There are many small pieces within a clock. The intricate coordination of these multiple pieces makes the clock function accurately. In my life, there are many small pieces, each valuable to me. When coordinated, they ensure the proper functioning of the whole. Today let me appreciate each small piece of my life and the intricate coordination that keeps them functioning smoothly.

15

The lotus flower is a symbol of contentment. Its quiet beauty floats serenely on the water, untouched by the mud below the surface. In meditation, I can experience a state of mind untouched by the mud of the world around me. This happens when I keep my thinking above the dirt but use the compost offered by the world to nourish my inner learning journey. Today let me live like a lotus.

16

Simplicity is a clean white background upon which a splash of colour can be seen. When I maintain a clean uncomplicated state of mind, I am more able to see beauty. Turning my attention away from over-thinking, I discover a simple clean space inside myself. This white space is the screen of consciousness that exists behind the thoughts and feelings projected onto it. By focusing on the screen, not the thoughts, I create simplicity. Today let me maintain a clean state of mind and enjoy splashes of beauty.

17

Newness begins in the mind. With a single thought, I can rearrange my entire view of the world. When my view is re-arranged, my feelings change, and I begin to see new angles in old relationships and situations. Then my interactions are renewed. Today let me create a new view.

18

Critical thinking leads me to find what is wrong in a situation. Although intended to be analytical, critical thinking focuses primarily on the negative. Positive thinking helps me discover what is right. Every situation has both positive and negative aspects to it. The positive is the life-giving part of any situation. When I choose a positive thinking lens, I choose to see what is 'right' or beautiful in order to grow it. By choosing to grow the positive, I give life to solutions. Today let me use a positive lens to look at the world.

19

The most powerful form of honesty is honesty with myself. Being honest with myself requires courage, determination and love. Courage gives me the strength to look in the places I avoid, determination keeps me from looking away and love softens my vision of myself. Today let me be honest.

20

You can't make old friends. Old friends grow with you. They watch you make mistakes and celebrate your successes. They mature alongside you. Old friends are companions on life's journey. They are cultivated, nourished and grown. Today let me recognize the special gift of old friends.

21

At the end of the day or after a physical workout, I kick off my shoes and put up my feet. In these moments when I am physically spent, I am often at my most content. Why? There is a connection between making effort and the deep satisfaction that allows me to fully relax afterwards. Contentment is an expression of deep satisfaction in the soul. Today let me appreciate and experience the secret of contentment ~ the satisfaction that comes with clean effort.

22

The ultimate expression of spirituality is a quality of character that is respectful and well-mannered. The sign that I have integrated the knowledge of myself as a peaceful spiritual being is my ability to treat myself and others with good manners. When not peaceful inside, I use force or subtle manipulation to get what I want. Spiritual awareness creates a powerful gentleness that allows me to treat every person with respect. Today let me express spiritual maturity with manners.

23

When my mind is weak, situations become a problem. When my mind is balanced, situations become a challenge. When my mind is strong, situations become opportunities. It's all a mind game. Today let me steady and strengthen my mind before I approach and handle situations.

24

Silence opens the mind to new possibilities. When I am involved with too many thoughts I get tossed around on a sea of inner turbulence. Silence is a lifeline out of this turbulence. Silence is an active state of inner power that enables me to focus on the horizon rather than get lost in the waves. Today let me enjoy moments of silence.

25

The most valuable part of the flower is the seed. If the seed is high quality and well-tended, a beautiful flower will grow. I can spend considerable time and energy watering each petal of my life and forget to care for the seed. The seed of me is the soul, the inner being. Caring for my inner being will ensure a beautiful expression as each leaf and petal of my life will benefit. Today let me enjoy the natural beauty that emerges when I care for the seed of me.

26

The world needs our hope and optimism. In a cynical world full of pessimism, it appears naïve to be hopeful and optimistic; a sure sign of being 'out of touch' with reality. However, the solutions needed for our world will not come from pessimism. Rather, they will come from hope, courage and positivity. Today let me offer the energy of hope and optimism as a gift to the world.

27

What keeps me strong when I feel frayed around the edges? Just as a well-used rope frays over time, I may fray on the surface, my energy going in all directions at the same time. Yet inside, my core strength is always there. To find it I must focus my attention inwards. Today let me remember my strength is always there at my core, even when I feel frayed.

28

A new world is created when I become new. As I apply my natural creative abilities to renewing myself, I begin to change. Then my world changes as a result. By turning old habits into new ones and creating new patterns, I begin to enjoy the process of creation and see how it affects my world. Today let me create newness in myself and transform my world.

29

My gift is the unique contribution I make to life. Because it is natural, and such an intrinsic part of me, I may not be able to see it. However, others can see my unique gift even if I cannot. Whether it is a sense of humour, a deep ability to care for others, the love of truth or the willingness to cooperate ~ it is a gift and it is intrinsic to who I am. Today let me recognize my gift and enjoy sharing it with the world.

30

In a world of constant movement, we take satisfaction from action. This can make it difficult to be still. Stillness is a natural balm for the soul, required for true rest. As I learn to meditate and concentrate my focus inwards, I begin to take satisfaction from stillness and silence. When this happens, I lose the compulsion to act. Then my actions are created by intention rather than compulsion. Today let me take satisfaction from stillness.

31

To live in the wrong tense is to become tense. Living in the future tense creates worry. Living in the past tense creates longing or regret. When I breathe life into the present moment, I open my heart to experience peace. Today let me live in the present tense.

FEBRUARY

1

Human hearts become parched and shrunken when living in a world of worry, pain and fear. Love can act like a soothing shower to quench the dryness of the spirit. Today let me replenish myself and others with spiritual love.

2

When a container is full it is stable and less likely to be knocked over. In the same way, when I am full I am less likely to be knocked over by life events. Stability comes when I am fully connected to my inner resources. I am stable when I draw strength from this inner reservoir of power. To stabilize myself in any situation I need only take a few moments to withdraw my attention from the outside world and anchor internally. Today let me be full and stable.

3

The soul experiences a sense of calm when there is order. When I lose inner power, my thoughts become chaotic and order is lost. I then seek to order my external world through control or structure. However order comes from the beauty and harmony inside the soul. Order comes with understanding. Order comes with cleanliness. Today let me focus on creating inner order and experience a sense of calm.

4

Doctors will not make me healthy. Nutritionists will not make me slim. Teachers will not make me smart. Gurus will not make me calm. Mentors will not make me rich. Trainers will not make me fit. Ultimately, I am responsible for the actions required to achieve any of these things. Today let me choose what I want and follow through with the small repeated actions required to make it happen.

5

When I leave home to explore the world, I take myself with me. No matter how independent I become, my strengths and weaknesses will come along as baggage. True independence comes when I conquer my weaknesses. A weakness compels me to act in ways that trap me in sorrow. The spiritual journey is one of liberation. True independence is to be free from the sorrow caused by my own weaknesses. Today let me become truly independent.

6

The sense organs are the antennae of the body. The intellect is the antennae of the soul. When my intellect is refined, I am able to detect the pure energy of peace, love, contentment, serenity and fulfillment. To enjoy this experience, I must reach beyond the world of noise and tune my intellect to the subtle frequency of silence. Today let me refine my intellect by tuning to the subtle.

7

Waste thoughts drain my inner power. A waste thought is an unproductive thought that takes my energy but gives nothing in return. The more thoughts I have the less power each thought contains. The fewer thoughts I have the more power each thought contains. When my thoughts are powerful, everything I create has more power in it and I experience more success. Today let me empower myself by increasing the quality of my thoughts.

8

I have a right to be the best version of myself. No one can give this to me because it already exists within me. I must claim my right to it or I will lose it. When I feel small, unworthy or challenged by criticism, I can remember that within me are all the qualities needed to respond well in every situation. Today let me reclaim my right to be my best self.

9

When I look at the imperfections of others, those same imperfections are activated in me. It is a secret of consciousness that I take on the energy of what I think about. Each time I think about a defect in someone else, I give it life inside of me. In the same way when I see virtues and specialties I activate my own good qualities. Today let me practice seeing the virtues and specialties in others, and fill myself with good energy.

10

A spider never gets caught in its own web. It can walk over each thread of its creation without getting stuck. In my life I create webs of connection. These can be glistening and beautiful, or they can be a trap. It all depends on my attitude towards my creation. When I am attached, I stick to the web and become entangled, losing my freedom and enjoyment. By holding a 'light touch' attitude in my mind towards my creation (my life, responsibilities, family, work) I am able to enjoy life without getting trapped. Today let me enjoy the beautiful web of my life.

11

My future is not determined ~ but I am. Although forecasts predict the weather, it is only my determined actions that will predict my future. With determination I will get to my destination. Determination allows me to face any weather and continue my journey towards my ultimate aim. Today let me be determined.

12

When I look at the world through a social justice lens, I see oppressors and oppressed. Through a psychological lens, I see victims and abusers. Through a spiritual lens I see 'beings' who want peace, but are trapped in old patterns of hurt and revenge, and numbed by materialism. I am able to see each person through the lens of respect and compassion, no matter how twisted their journey may seem. When I develop tolerance, I can respond with respect in every situation rather than aggression or anger. Today let me see the world through a spiritual lens and grow my capacity to tolerate and respect.

13

Silence and creativity are partners. A quiet mind relaxes me and allows me to concentrate. Then creativity flows. To increase creativity in my life, I must set the right conditions through silence. Today let me nourish creativity with silence.

14

Peace is the result of settling leftovers from the past. To make peace with myself and my story I must face and dissolve old wounds and regrets with the energy of forgiveness, realization and love. This reconciliation process brings me peace. After peace, silence follows. Today let me create peace through internal reconciliation.

15

My conscience keeps me on the straight and narrow. It can discern the rightness or wrongness of something as well as its trueness or falseness. Studies have shown that we go against our conscience several times each day. Usually in small matters such as doing something we know is not good for us. When I regularly go against my conscience, it ceases to function. When my conscience stops speaking to me, I experience confusion and make mistakes I will later regret. Today let me listen to my conscience.

16

If the weather makes me happy, it will also make me sad. Cold or grey climates can affect a person's mood. It can be a challenge to stay happy in spite of the weather. Although, even with the sun it is possible to be unhappy. Generating happiness begins by looking inwards and recognizing that my inner climate can be independent of the weather. Today let me smile regardless of the weather.

17

There is a Japanese idea that to go fast is to move slowly ~ without interruption. Time is the space between actions. In a world of activity, there is little space between actions and therefore the feeling that I have no time. Paradoxically when I move more slowly, time expands and more gets done. Today let me move slowly, steadily, with dignity and enjoy more time.

18

Pure gold is malleable and never tarnishes. When another metal is added, gold becomes heavy and less flexible. Like gold, I have mixed within me the remnants of memories, hurts and losses from life's journey. This can make me rigid, fixed in certain attitudes and postures of mind. Just as alloy is removed from gold with heat, I can dissolve the leftovers from life with the heat of determination and the purifying rays of the Spiritual Sun. Today let me remember that negative energy can be removed with determination and love.

19

The ears hear ~ the soul listens. The eyes see ~ the soul observes. The mouth tastes ~ the soul enjoys. The nose smells ~ the soul experiences. The hands touch ~ the soul feels. Today let me be aware that I am the living, human spirit who experiences life from inside a human body through the five senses.

20

I can live life as if it is fixed in my favour. I can choose to think that my future will turn out well. A positive attitude opens doorways and creates possibilities. I still need to make effort to move in a positive direction. With the consistent practice of a positive attitude, and doing the 'work' required, life opens its arms and welcomes me. Today let me choose an attitude of hope and optimism.

21

A spiritual rose is someone who is able to stay in the midst of thorns, yet remains loving and detached. In a world of thorns, it is easy to be pricked and to become prickly. I make the choice to be like a rose by protecting myself from the thorns, within and around me. As a rose, I find ways to bring beauty and the fragrance of peace, love and respect to all situations. Today let me be a rose.

22

When I feel powerless, ego pushes me to assert myself as better, bigger or stronger than others. This dangerous game guarantees that I will receive the karmic return by continuing to feel powerless. Only by stepping out of this vicious cycle and acknowledging my vulnerability will I find the spiritual strength to be gentle and honest. Today let me be spiritually powerful and refuse to play ego's games.

23

When I am afraid of an obstacle, it has power over me. When I see the obstacle for what it really is, a life lesson designed to strengthen me, I become bigger than even the most fierce thing in front of me. My change of awareness gives me the power to detach from fear. Then I can smile and see the obstacle as a paper tiger, knowing I will conquer it. Today let me conquer obstacles by changing my awareness.

24

Each experience in my life is like a thread woven into the fabric of my heart. The quality of my heart is determined by the quality of these threads. Hard or challenging situations serve to strengthen my heart. Love and generosity open my heart. Each thread of experience adds to my heart. Today let me be aware of the quality of my heart.

25

Light distinguishes day from night. Away from the equator, when the days are shorter and the nights longer, people wait with anticipation for the light to return. At this time in the world, all souls are seeking light. Whatever the tradition or belief system, everyone wants to experience light. Spiritual light is the inner flame of the soul lit with the pure energy of self-awareness. Today let me sparkle brightly and add light to the world.

26

When I have a clear aim, I am inspired to achieve it. The more I love my aim, the greater will be my determination to continue in the face of challenges and storms. My aim makes me strong and determined. When I keep my aim in front of me, it will inspire me to keep going. Today let me remember my aim and take strength from it.

27

The conscience is the subtle inner voice that distinguishes right from wrong in every situation. My conscience is more discerning than the 'morality' of the day. This means that something considered 'right' in my social context may not be right for me. When I listen to my conscience, it functions well. If I have silenced my conscience it will be difficult to hear. Then I become confused and easily influenced by the peer pressure of my social setting. Today let me listen to my conscience and do what is right for me.

28

Computers have a spam filter to redirect junk mail. Like a computer, my mind receives input from many directions; from people, the media, and my own subconscious memories. Much of this information is like spam and clogs my mind. On a daily basis I can clean my mind with a spam filter by redirecting useless thoughts to the trash bin. This frees space for more valuable information. Today let me use my spam filter to delete unnecessary information from my mind.

29

An extra day, an unexpected bonus, a chance to add something special to my life and my world this year. Today let me take stock and appreciate the abundance I have within me, in my relationships and in my life.

MARCH

1

When my foundation is strong, the storms of life do not rock me. The light of a lighthouse will only be seen if its foundation is strong and built to withstand the crashing ocean. For my light to shine, I need a strong inner foundation, built on a regular practice of silence and spiritual study. Today let me strengthen my foundation so my light can be seen.

2

Anger burns relationships. When awakened, old habits of irritation, impatience and anger burn me inside. With moments of reflection and meditation I can learn to calm this old habit. By using acceptance, love and the coolness of peace, I can regain perspective. Then with firm determination I can move beyond anger. Today let me be cool.

3

We live in a world that feeds violence. For non-violence to exist, it must be fed by something very powerful. Violence can ignite an inner battle between my innate peace and the lower animal instincts fed by the world. Peace is a power greater than violence. When experienced, peace automatically slows me down and creates non-violent thoughts, words and actions. Today let me experience the power of peace and become truly non-violent.

4

Expansion is fascinating, Essence is breathtaking. My mind is involved in the expansion of details all day, roaming from idea to idea in a never-ending explosion of associations. Like a soap-opera, expansion captivates until it exhausts. The act of focusing my mind in a pinpoint of concentrated awareness is to experience 'essence'. It is breath-taking. Today let me focus my awareness on the essence.

5

It's not the load that breaks me, it's how I carry it. Carrying a load in an unbalanced way can make me fall. 'Carrying' a responsibility with fear or resentment will break my spirit. I find the right balance when I hold a responsibility lightly and with dignity. Keeping my eyes focused forward, I maintain a steady pace towards my goal. Today let me carry my responsibilities in a balanced way.

6

Everything I see around me is first experienced in my mind. Although the eyes serve as instruments through which light bounces and images are formed, it is in the mind that I interpret what I see. It is important to check what is in my mind during the day. Not all that I see needs to be considered or experienced. I can choose what to allow into my mind and ensure that I interpret it with care. Today let me check what is in my mind.

7

The lotus flower sits royal and beautiful above the mud. Although the mud is not beautiful, it provides the ideal conditions for the lotus to grow. In the same way, it is possible that my present circumstances (including the not so beautiful aspects) are ideal for my spiritual growth. Today let me consider and appreciate my growth-supporting environment.

8

Each person has a unique path, one they alone can follow. Although I may travel with others on the spiritual journey, our roads will bend and turn in different directions. How do I find my own path? I follow the subtle signals in my heart and listen to my longings. I pay attention to signals that reveal open doorways, where others see only walls. Today let me stay tuned to the subtle signals of my own path.

9

The ocean floor is silent and still. Pebbles at the bottom of the ocean do not move much. Although there are crashing waves at the surface, the world at the bottom is silent and still. On the surface of my mind, there are thoughts and feelings crashing like the waves on the ocean. If I take a moment to go deeper, I will discover silence and stillness. Today let me dive into my mind and find the depth of peace.

10

Perfect balance is found when two strengths come together. When a weakness attempts to balance itself with a strength, the result is known as compensation not balance. The most stable balance is created when two strengths come together to complement and reinforce each other. Today let me express my strengths in balance.

11

When a person lacks inner power they will seek a powerful position, often over others. It's not the position title that makes me powerful, it is how I hold myself in that position. When I feel powerful inside, I hold my head high with humility and self-respect. I am able to be kind, gentle and generous because I have nothing to prove and no one to impress. Today let me hold myself in an inner position of self-respect and serve well in any position.

12

The silent whisper of my inner voice can only be heard if I listen closely. Intuitively I know what is best for me and what is best in every situation. The inner voice of my conscience, my higher wisdom, will never leave or deceive me. But I have to listen very carefully to hear its wisdom. It will not yell above the noise of my mind when filled with other voices telling me what to do. It can only be heard in silence. Today let me listen to myself.

13

Water finds its way around all obstacles. It flows around and past anything that gets in its way. It stops to gather enough volume to push the obstacle out of the way or to get past it. In the same way, when obstacles come into my life, they provide an opportunity for me to stop and build strength before carrying on. Today let me be like water, gathering strength to flow around all obstacles.

14

The 'detached observer' practice is the act of stepping back slightly from the situation or person I am interacting with. This 'stepping back' happens in my mind and creates a small mental space between myself and the other, giving me a chance to see clearly. It creates a protective distance, an emotional buffer, in which to check my reactions and transform them into the most accurate and elevated response. Today let me create a little respectful space between myself and the world.

15

Every thought is like a drop of paint on the canvas of my life. Each thought adds colour and texture to the picture. Negative thoughts add dark or muddy colours to the picture. Positive thoughts add bright, cheery colours. The final creation will be beautiful when I choose thoughts that give meaning and beauty to my existence. Today let me colour my life well.

16

There are no bad people, only good people who do bad things when they are weak. Sometimes I do not have the inner power, the moral courage, the discipline or strength to do what I know is right. When this happens, I lose respect for myself. It requires inner power to do what is right, even when it is hard. I gather this inner spiritual power through meditation, reflection and by reconnecting with my core spiritual energy. Today let me restore my self-respect by accumulating inner power.

17

The way I do anything is the way I do everything. How I brush my teeth, peel potatoes or make my bed is an expression of my character. The way I take care of the small ordinary things in life is a reflection of my relationship with myself, and an indicator of how I take care of the big things in life. Today let me take care of the little things with care.

18

There is no sense to the senses. The senses detect that which is physical. Sense, on the other hand, is based on understanding and wisdom. The senses don't make sense of a situation, they bring data in from the outside world to be processed by the subtle, metaphysical soul. Today let me use my senses for the physical world and my subtle spiritual awareness to make sense of my experiences.

19

People go to temples, mosques and churches to experience sacred space. These places are sacred because they have been filled with thoughts of love, respect and attention to the highest in humanity and to the Divine. I can create a sacred space in my home by giving attention to the highest and best through cleanliness, quiet moments of reflection, meditation and connection to the sacred. Today let me create a sacred space in my home.

20

The social construction of identity means that I am who I think I am because others have told me this is who I am. Identity, in today's world, is often based on the body ~ my gender, my skin color, my bodily size or shape. When I meditate, I recognize myself as the quiet subtle energy that lives in a body. In a time when identity polarizes people, this spiritual vision is the most inclusive vision we can have of others. Inside the body, independent of color, size, gender or nationality, is a human spirit. Today let me expand my awareness beyond the body and relate to others through a spiritual identity.

21

Doors come in many colors and sizes. Inside of me there are many doors ~ a door to softness, openness, courage, honesty and many other virtues. Which door do I wish to open inside myself today? Intention and awareness are the keys to open every door. Today let me open new doors in myself.

22

There is something uniquely mesmerizing about the line that marks the meeting between sea and sky. The vastness of each entity stirs the spirit and awakens an awe for nature's majesty. I am reminded of the vast potential stored within me. Today let me greet my unlimited potential.

23

The company I keep colors me. The conversation and energy of a social gathering can have a positive or negative effect on me. When I am with good company I feel good. Then I wonder how to make myself 'color fast' so it doesn't wash away in the rain of negative energy. Today let me appreciate good company and hold positive energy within me.

24

Only when I begin to clean something do I notice how dirty it is. A thin layer of dust evenly coating a surface is not visible until the surface is wiped. In the same way, dirt settles in the soul in the form of energy absorbed from outside. I experience this inner dirt as heaviness or an off-mood. It clogs my mind making it difficult to see or feel clearly. A regular cleaning is necessary to reveal what I have accumulated. Today let me create a regular cleaning practice to remove the dust collected during the day.

25

Each time I make a fashion choice I am using my body to express my inner qualities. Each choice of clothing can represent a quality of my personality. Perhaps it is cleanliness I am expressing, or simplicity, elegance or dignity. What is the quality I am expressing today through my choice of clothing?

26

There comes a time when the soul wants to go home; home to peace, home to my true self. This is known as the spiritual pilgrimage. It is a silent internal matter of the heart and mind, not a physical trek across landscapes. The yearning for peace, love and silence becomes so great that I must travel beyond the physical to find them. Then I discover meditation, solitude, contemplation and reflection and rediscover the pathway back home to myself. Today let me honour my deep desire to come home to myself.

27

There is a great sense of joy when my attention is absorbed in stillness. In a world of constant movement and distraction, it feels luxurious to be still. Yet this luxury is necessary for the health of my mind. Today let me dedicate time to the luxury of focusing my attention inwards to stillness.

28

My energy becomes fixed when I have a strong opinion or preference. This rigidity creates a wall against which other energies are experienced as attacks or opposition. When my energy is flexible, I easily flow with situations and people to create solutions that work for all. Today let me soften my own energy and dissolve walls.

29

The economy shrinks when everyone takes. Only by giving will we kick-start the economy again. When I generate the spirit of giving (my time, my attention, my care), I help activate the highest human quality of generosity and benevolence. This becomes contagious and is ultimately returned which leads to a sense of abundance. Today let me grow the economy by giving.

30

When you build a house, every brick counts. When you build a character, every thought counts. Who I am comes from what I think. Thoughts that build the highest quality character are based on love, purity, peace and wisdom. The more my thoughts are filled with these qualities, the more my character is shaped around them. Today let me think high quality thoughts.

31

A paintbrush, when dipped in water, absorbs the pigment of paint. My mind is like a brush, absorbing the energy (colour) of anything it touches. When I 'touch' something by thinking about it for a long period of time, I absorb its energy. Being aware of this process means I can choose the colours I wish to absorb. Today let me carefully select the colour of energy I will absorb.

APRIL

1

Happiness is generative. It is experienced as an abundance of good feelings. To be happy, I must accumulate pure karma. Giving is the karma that increases my happiness. Today let me generate happiness through pure intentions and actions.

2

To change the world we must first change our minds. All great inventions begin in the mind. The mind follows a picture. To live simply, peacefully and happily I must create pictures of simplicity, peace and happiness in my mind first. When I can see these, I will be able to create them. Then my life will become an example that inspires others. Today let me change my mind.

3

Sunflowers are 'heliotropic' or sun-seeking. They turn their large faces throughout the day to continually face the sun. When I commit to a life lived in the light, I commit to drawing only the energy that nourishes the soul. I choose to turn my attention away from darkness, not as denial, but like a sunflower, to stay in the light of positive influences. Today let me be like a sunflower and face the Light.

4

Two indicators of spiritual transformation are: worry reduces and one becomes more lighthearted and joyful. Also a person begins to see more meaningful coincidences and moments of synchronicity in life. To what extent do I see these indicators in my spiritual growth? What other indicators do I see? Today let me notice the signs of my own transformation.

5

When I promise something for the future, I postpone the opportunity to give in the present moment. As life unfolds, events may prevent me from giving at the 'promised' time, in spite of my deep integrity and commitment. When I approach each moment as the only certain moment to give, then I will give now and not delay. Today let me give in this moment.

6

Life is better when you are happy. But life is at its best when other people are happy because of you! When I am happy I can give happiness to others. Today let me give happiness and be happy.

7

The butterfly flies because it has let go of its caterpillar life. Before becoming a butterfly, the caterpillar passes through a stage of voracious eating which fuels the time spent in the chrysalis. On my spiritual journey, I too experience the appetite for spiritual input and enlightened ideas. For transformation to occur, I must use this valuable input as fuel for silent periods of solitude. This internal process may not be visible externally, but it is felt as a period of deep inner quiet. In solitude, I shed the old me, based on conditioned responses and old stories and the REAL me emerges, free as a butterfly. Today let me feed inner transformation with solitude.

8

Sweet relations between us are based on the ability to truly 'see' the other person. To really see someone for who they are, beyond the packaging of the body, the fashion style, the opinions and lifestyle practices ~ is to see the soul. Beneath the layers we are all peaceful beings. World peace is a result of this elevated vision. Today let me see everyone as a soul.

9

Trees provide a beautiful canopy under which we live as human beings. The canopy of a tree provides protection from the wind, rain and sun. Trees generate life-giving oxygen and remove carbon monoxide from the air. Trees generate elements required for living. They protect life. Today let me be like a tree and offer life-giving spiritual sustenance to those around me while providing a canopy of protection from negative elements.

10

We collect possessions like clothes, books, furniture, and other things. At some point my closets become full of unused items and I find myself living in a cluttered environment. I can also become cluttered spiritually, with a collection of worries, doubts and sorrow. I can clean my spiritual clutter in the same way a good spring cleaning helps me declutter my physical closets. To clean my inner closets, I must let go of emotional baggage and rearrange my thinking to a higher, more spiritual level. Today let me clean my inner closets and free myself from spiritual and emotional clutter.

11

When the energy in my voice comes from the core of my spirit, its expression is genuine and captivating. It compels others to listen. The world supports spontaneous, true expression. When I speak, do I ensure that my words come from the depth of my inner reservoir of truth? When they do, they will be heard. Today let me speak with truth.

12

The world is full of thorns, spikes, prickly people and sticky situations. It is sometimes difficult to see the best bits, the life-giving core of a situation or person. However, like a bee who knows how to get the nectar from even the prickliest plant, I can develop my capacity to see and take only the best bits. This requires the knowledge that nectar is found beneath the surface. Although outer layers may appear ugly, there is always something positive and life-giving at the core. Even the most negative situation can act as a catalyst to bring the best out in me. Today let me discover the positive in every situation.

13

When I encounter ego in myself I can dissolve it with acceptance, kindness, and respect. If I react to ego with force, aggression or impatience, it grows. Today let me dissolve ego with kindness.

14

Relatives are people with whom I share a genetic biological connection. When I define myself 'relative' to another, thinking I am a father, a daughter, a cousin, etc., I limit my connections. As a soul I am in relationship with many people and I share qualities and close connections with many people other than my relatives. At a spiritual level, we all share One Spiritual Parent, making everyone my brother or sister. Today let me relate to everyone as part of my spiritual family.

15

Honesty makes it possible to see my specialties as well as my weaknesses. When I am able to see myself with appreciation and compassion, I develop a loving attitude towards myself. This softens my vision of others. Then my ability and capacity to love grows. Today let me be lovingly honest with myself.

16

There can only be peace of mind when the heart is happy. The feelings in my heart drive the thoughts in my mind. When the heart is hurt, the mind is distressed. To soothe and calm my heart I must access the spiritual love at my core and draw love from the Divine Source. Then my mind becomes calm and peaceful. Today let me soothe my heart and bring peace to my mind.

17

The energy of thinking is precious. When collected, it can be channeled and used to create a quality life. When my thought energy is scattered I am unable to concentrate and act effectively or efficiently. Casting a mental net outwards, I can pull my thought energy into a concentrated still point. Collecting thought energy gives me power. Today let me collect my precious energy of thought with the net of determination.

18

When the soul is tired, the body is heavy. When the mind is cluttered, the body is fatigued. Sometimes we sleep to escape soul weariness. When I am happy and expressing my gift, I am not tired, I am energized. Today let me find a way to replenish the soul and watch my body become lighter.

19

In major cities around the world, tall architectural structures stand as notable landmarks. In times past, these buildings were churches, temples and mosques. Now, they are office buildings. Regardless of their intention, these impressive structures draw our gaze upwards, following the peak of the building to the sky beyond. Pyramids are said to represent rays of light descending from the heavens, a pathway between the physical and spiritual worlds. Looking up, I am reminded of places and things beyond the material world. Today let me look up in wonder.

20

Focus on growth and that which is not growing will fall away. If I want to grow something new inside myself, I must shift the focus of my energy and attention away from the old. I must stop trying to fix or manage a weakness. Instead when I put all my energy into growing a new habit, the old habit naturally falls away. Today let me focus on growth.

21

Art is soul-expression. The desire to create is a natural expression of the soul. We each have our form of creative expression. Spiritually I can paint my life with the colour of beauty and joy. I can sing a melody of kindness and peace or sculpt a world shaped with love. I can draw mental lines that contrast light and dark or I can dance in my mind to create a golden future. Today let me find a way to express my creative energy.

22

I lose my balance when I judge others. My own imperfections emerge when I look at the imperfections of those around me. Only when I respect myself will I be able to respect others. Respecting others helps me respect myself. Today let me maintain the elegant balance of self-respect and giving respect to others.

23

Sometimes I get caught up in thinking I am the sum of everything I do, that my actions define me. By getting caught up in worrying about each of my actions and its impact, I forget about who I am. When I remember I am a BEING of peace, my actions will be filled with the peaceful energy of my being. Then my pure intentions will carry each action to a positive outcome. Today let me remember who I truly am - a human being not a human doing.

24

Bloom where you are planted. Life has a way of planting me in situations that are beneficial for my growth. Some situations prune me back where I am expanding in a way that disperses my life energy. Other situations nourish me deeply, enabling me to express the colour of my inner beauty. When I appreciate the gift each situation offers for my growth, I relax into the simple task of blossoming. This is my only task ~ to bloom. Today let me enjoy life in my inner garden.

25

Optimism is the lens through which I look at the world. Like a kaleidoscope that arranges bits of colored glass into a pleasing view, I can choose to organize the bits of my life into a view that pleases. The energy of optimism is the organizing principle of positivity. Today let me apply the lens of optimism to arrange the bits of my life into a pleasing view.

26

Fixed lines of loyalty and kinship often define who we are willing to help. Historical and tribal boundaries are crossed when there is need. When extreme difficulties occur, people reach beyond the comfort of their perimeter (neighbourhood, race or culture) to help others. It is uplifting and inspiring to witness this and feeds a growing sense of unity in our human family. Today let me stretch my heart and mind beyond my zone of comfort.

27

If I admit a mistake immediately, half of it is erased from my memory. This is due to the resolution that comes from acknowledgment. However, a trace will be left in my memory track and stored away. In moments when I feel weak, these memories will flood into my mind and provide justification for a lack of self-respect. Today let me admit mistakes and strengthen my foundation of self-respect for the future.

28

To see life through the lens of black/white, right/wrong, my way/your way, is to be trapped in polarity. Between polarities, there are subtle threads that tie opposing energies together, helping them blend and integrate. When I see these threads I am able to stand between polarities and become a third way. Today let me be a thread of unity that integrates polarity.

29

As children, we create as easily as we breathe. I began life with many passions that inspired and ignited my imagination. Slowly my interests reduced as my energy was channeled into duties and responsibilities. As an adult, do I know my interests? It is when I follow my interests that I discover who I am. Today let me honour and explore my interests.

30

"Attitude creates atmosphere." Dadi Janki (Administrative Head of the Brahma Kumaris)

Attitude is everything. It creates the atmosphere around me. The awareness I hold in my mind, creates an attitude. This attitude is expressed through my vibrations, my vision and my actions. I can tell when the atmosphere of a place is lovely and I wish to spend time there or when it is stale, negative or heavy. Today let me set an attitude that is life-giving and create a beautiful atmosphere wherever I go.

MAY

1

When I think about peace, I create a still pool of peaceful energy inside me. This pool of peace extends outward to the world. Even if a stone is thrown, I can easily return to my inner reservoir of peace. Today let me create a pool of peaceful energy.

2

When an obstacle comes into my life, I feel like I have lost my freedom. I enslave myself to the obstacle by thinking 'I will be free when this obstacle finishes', or 'when my relatives change' or 'when those who create obstacles for me stop creating obstacles'. In realty I must be determined to free myself first, then the obstacle will disappear. The rock will still be in the road, but it will be behind me because I was determined to get around it. When obstacles come, my freedom relies on my determination to find a way. Today let me find a way to free myself from obstacles.

3

The energy of life is always moving and changing. Life's gifts come and go, creating space for new gifts. I suffer when I try to hold life in one place. Today let me flow with life's changing energy.

4

Beware of telling stories about other people that let me off the hook. When I take 100 per cent responsibility for myself I can see that my life has been my creation. The choices I made ~ to get involved, not get involved, to stay, to leave ~ have created my life as it is. No one else is to blame. To tell stories about others is to hide from taking responsibility for my choices. Today let me be honest with myself and shape my life truthfully.

5

In the symphony of life, we all have a part to play. For the music to be harmonious and beautiful, each one must play their own part well. What is my part? What am I an instrument for? Love? Enthusiasm? Generosity? Taking the time to truly understand my part makes it possible for me to share my special gifts for the benefit of others. Today let me play my part in life's symphony and add to its rich harmony.

6

It is not self-centered to get yourself centered. Many of us feel guilty when we take time alone to recharge. The best way to centre myself is to stop for a brief moment and be in the centre of everything that is going on around me. By stopping and just observing all that is happening, I find the centre still-point of myself and experience a respite from the storm. Today let me centre myself.

7

My mind is a precious place. It will be filled with the energy I allow inside. My mind can be like a temple or a dustbin. Sweet, pure honest thoughts fill my mind with beautiful energy. When I understand the power I have to determine the quality of energy in my mind, I will only allow entry to those thoughts that fill it with beauty. Today let me treat my mind as a sacred space.

8

A dancer stands in front of a mirror to self-correct. Tiny adjustments, made day after day, result in a perfect form and create movement that is beautiful to watch. In the same way, this exquisite accuracy is used in spiritual practice. Many times each day I can check my consciousness and reset it to peace, self-respect and love. I self-correct by adjusting my attitude and intentions to their purest expression. Today let me self-correct in little steps and dance with life.

9

Although Monarch butterflies migrate alone, they cluster in cold weather. This is a protection against predators who are more able to see them when there is no foliage. In the same way, we human beings, flutter about on our solo journeys until the cold of a world crisis pulls us together. We seek comfort and protection with others. It is time for us to cluster, to stay close together and to offer each other comfort and protection. Today let me stay close to humanity.

10

A life lived with the purpose of bringing benefit to others creates a feeling of richness and abundance inside. My heart is fulfilled when I give. Then I don't need many material possessions to be happy. Today let me give and live a rich fulfilling life.

11

People with dementia store recent experiences as feelings, not facts. Conversations cannot be fact-based because only the feelings remain. It is the same with the soul. Although I cannot remember the detailed facts of all my past experiences, the feelings they have left are vivid and can be provoked at any time. Without wasting time or energy trying to identify the source, I can honour the existence of the feeling. Then I can gently redirect my mind towards a more positive feeling. Today let me honour my feelings.

12

When I am a guest I am usually on holiday, away from my regular routines and responsibilities. On holiday, I have a lot of energy as I am not drained by the feeling of responsibility or burden. Even mundane activities, like making meals become more fun as a guest. When I adopt the attitude of being a guest in my life, I begin to enjoy the extra energy that comes from being "on holiday". Today let me experiment with the consciousness of being a guest.

13

Force is an energy that creates resistance. Power is an energy that attracts. Ego uses my inner power to force people or situations to do as I say or want. Even subtle attempts to manipulate are ego's work. This creates resistance and depletes cooperation. When I use my inner power to let go of control, I begin to see the natural direction in which a situation is flowing. By going with the flow, I create harmony. Today let me use my inner power to attract cooperation.

14

Self-love is the ability to look in the mirror and see the soul behind the eyes. No matter what mistakes I am making, I know I am a spiritual being, doing my best and I am striving to learn, grow and do better. Today let me offer myself love and appreciation.

15

There is a difference between love and attachment. Love *never* hurts, attachment does. When I am attached, I am dependent on someone or something. I *need* them to be present for me to feel complete. When they leave, I am empty. Although romanticized, this is not love. This is dependency. When love is mixed with attachment it becomes possessive and I weaken myself and the other person. Love wants what is best for another, even if it takes them away from me. Love supports and empowers both people. Love is a gift that uplifts. Today let me recognize the difference between attachment and love and grow the love in all my relationships.

16

When confused, I delay action until I have clarity. Sometimes it is the consistent repetition of small, positive actions that will create clarity. When confusion reigns, inertia and inactivity can feed it. My decision to act, with even the smallest action, serves as a catalyst for clarity. Today let me choose to take small, positive steps and trust that complete clarity will follow.

17

Silence is a very good mental teacher. It teaches me how to listen and how to hear. It teaches me to discern how I feel and articulate these feelings in words. Silence allows me to go deeper inside to find the peace that surpasses understanding. It makes peace possible by allowing me to experience myself as a silent being. Today I will learn the art of silence.

18

Staying true to myself is like walking on a balance beam. Distractions and reactions attempt to pull me off-balance, away from my centre point of equilibrium. I lose my dignity when I lose my balance. Maintaining balance requires constant attention. With love, determination and inner power I can stay focused and true on the balance beam of life. Today let me experience the sheer joy of staying true to myself.

19

When I make a mistake, ego makes me defensive, preventing me from learning valuable lessons. When I resolve to learn from my mistakes, I conquer ego. Even if 99% of a mistake involves another person, I can first be honest with myself and see what part I played. Only then can I learn. By becoming a humble learner, I free myself from ego. Today let me bypass ego to gain wisdom from my mistakes and accelerate my self-development.

20

The more attachments I have (to ideas, people or places), the more obstacles will come into my path. When I am holding onto something, I become inflexible and rigid. When rigid, I bump into life. I am unable to bend and flow with it and begin to experience my life filled with obstacles. Today let me release attachment and flow with life.

21

Children put their hands over their eyes when they don't want to see something scary. I may also refuse to see something I don't want to see in myself. Without the desire to see clearly, I live inside a blind spot. Others can see what is invisible to me. This is an uncomfortable way to live, as I bump into difficulties caused by the blind spot. When I face these dark spots with courage and honesty, I will find the tools and insight to transform them. Today let me face the parts of myself I would like to transform.

22

As my spiritual strength increases, I give up the habit of worrying. Worry serves no purpose but makes me feel tense and miserable. When I stop fretting about things that are beyond my control, I am able to focus on generating optimistic and kind thoughts. Then my life begins to flow in more positive constructive directions. Today let me adopt a light and easy approach to life.

23

Contentment is not about having everything I want, it is about appreciating what I have. It only takes a moment to shift my attitude. Then I suddenly see the beauty of my situation, of what I have, of who I am. The ability to shift my attitude requires practice. At first, it feels mechanical and a bit clumsy. Over time, I retrain my thinking and rewire my brain until appreciation becomes my immediate response and a way of life. Today let me appreciate what I have and be content.

24

My subconscious mind is full of self-images stored as memories from the past. Some of these images are positive and inspiring. Others are limiting, tying me to a reality of myself that is old and outdated. My self-awareness influences everything I do and say. Using the power of my imagination, I can create positive images of myself as I would like to be. When I hold these not-yet-realized images in my awareness, my subconscious mind accepts them. Over time, this awareness becomes reality. Today let me create images of me at my best.

25

Fear of facing my weaknesses prevents me from being honest with myself. It also prevents me from seeing my strengths. Today let me face my weaknesses so I can also see my strengths.

26

There comes a time when you have to choose between turning the page or closing the book. How do I know whether to continue with something or step away from it? To stay too long is to invite stagnation; to leave too quickly is to miss an opportunity for depth and learning. If I am open, signals are always there to guide me on my journey. Today let me pay attention to subtle signals and discern the most life-giving choice.

27

When the world is burning in anger and greed, the energy of peace and tolerance acts like water to cool it down. Responding with anger or greed only feeds the flames and prolongs the fire. Coolness comes with thoughts of acceptance and respect. Today let me be a fire brigade and respond to heated situations or people with the coolness of peace and tolerance.

28

It is a luxury to live as if you can put things off. When I live in this 'luxury of eventually' I postpone important things. Even those things near and dear to my heart drift to the bottom of my priority list if I am not paying careful attention. Eventually I discover that I have not given my best to what matters most to me. Today let me seize the day and give attention to my most important people, dreams and actions.

29

Sometimes it is important to push gently against a door to open new opportunities. Other times, no matter how hard it is pushed, the door will not open. Then I understand this is not my door. How do I know the difference? Sometimes a little extra effort is required and I must rally my determination and strength. But when I begin to use force, it is a sign that this is not my door. The energy of force is different than determination and perseverance. Today let me check, is this my door?

30

Patience is an expression of peace. When I use the peace within me as a power, it allows me to be patient. Patience is also supported by an understanding that everything ripens in its own time. Fruit will be destroyed if forced to ripen too quickly. In the same way, forcing a situation to move too fast will destroy its natural unfolding. Today let me practice patience.

31

How do you find your way home in the desert? In the desert, there are landmarks and signals recognizable only to those who know the terrain. In the same way, each of us has our own life journey with signals that are recognizable only to us. To find my way home to myself I must follow the subtle internal signals of my intuition, insight and instincts. Today let me follow my internal compass home.

JUNE

1

When I've done something wrong, it is best to admit it and be sorry. Holding onto a mistake or denying it will only make it grow like a stain in my consciousness. With humility, I see that I will not choke by swallowing my pride. In fact, I will feel clean inside and ready to try again. Today let me face mistakes with honesty and lightness.

2

We live in a world of multiple priorities. A priority is, by definition, only one. With so many priorities it is hard to know where to focus my attention and easy to forget what is most important to me. When my attention is fragmented, my energy is dispersed. When I have one singular focus, it is easy to remember and I am able to concentrate my energy. What is the ONE thing I want to remember every day? It might be peace or God or compassion or kindness. Today let me decide what is most important to me, and focus my energy and attention on it.

3

The seed of my future begins in this moment. The quality of energy I put into the 'now' determines the quality of my future. The choices I make now set the pathway for future choices and return. The best way to create a good future is by giving high quality energy to the present. Today let me give, live, love NOW and create a beautiful future.

4

I lose my peace when I give my mind to peace-less things, like the news or troubling stories. Each time I engage with negative energy I give away control of my mind. To reclaim my mind, I must turn away from negativity. This does not mean I deny or suppress bad news. I acknowledge it, then turn my attention to something that makes me feel positive and hopeful. When I fill my mind with positive energy, I can then offer it to the world. Today let me reclaim my mind.

5

There is a silence into which the world cannot intrude. There is an ancient peace I carry in my heart, and have not lost. This is an inner sanctuary so deep that it has never been touched by the world outside. A memory of this 'place' remains with me always. When the longing to return intensifies, I will find my way back. Today let me come back to my peace.

6

Bamboo trees have multiple individual roots. When one bamboo stalk rubs against another they can spark on fire. Sandalwood, on the other hand, is a multi-branched tree with one set of roots. When sandalwood branches rub together they create a beautiful fragrance, used in incense sticks and cooling paste. Spirituality reminds me of the common roots of humanity. When I feel separate from others, my reactions can flare and cause conflict. When I see the common roots of my human family, I seek to bring out the best in everyone. Then my relationships become fragrant, like sandal-wood. Today let me honour shared roots.

7

When trees stand too close to each other, the sun cannot enter the forest. When trees stand separate, but beside each other, the sun can shine into the space between them. Growth occurs when there is space and light in my relationships. Today let me create space.

8

In every situation, something is finishing and something is beginning. For newness to be created, the old must end. This is the nature of transformation. I can ask myself: *what am I being called to keep alive in this situation?* Sometimes the aspect I want to keep alive is the part that needs to die in order for there to be new growth. Sometimes I am being called to keep alive the power of hope, peace or civility in the midst of breakdown. Today let me focus on keeping the right things alive.

9

In solitude, I can breathe deeply and take a break from the noise and action of the world. This replenishes my body and soul. In solitude, I accumulate a reserve of inner silence. With the oxygen of solitude, I am able to give others the breath of courage. To give courage to someone is to give them the breath of life, encouraging them to be strong and carry on. Today let me practice solitude and replenish my spiritual breath.

10

Our connection with Mother Nature is very intimate. Our bodies consist of her five elements. Our love for nature unites us across religions, nationalities and even politics. Mother Nature is suffering from the effects of human intervention. While political solutions are blocked by ego, I can reach out with my heart and mind to soothe and protect her. Today let me offer my deepest love and regard to Mother Nature.

11

I carry inside me the wonders I seek outside. Each experience and relationship I have awakens something in me. I may attribute these qualities to the 'other' rather than to myself. I may not acknowledge the qualities they have awakened in me. Every experience and relationship activates something in me. Today let me honour the wonders inside of me.

12

How do we make a difference in the world at this time? Expressing anger and outrage will create even more anger and outrage. Suppressing anger will result in a blow up, often when least expected. Repressing anger will eventually make me sick. I must transform feelings of anger, vengeance and powerlessness into the qualities I want to see in the world. When I speak with clarity and positivity about what I want I create images that help others see. Then we walk together with conviction to create a better world by bringing the needed qualities into being. Today let me make a difference in the world by creating what is needed.

13

Spiritual energy is unseen. It can only be perceived by a subtle intellect that can see beyond the surface veil to the invisible truth hidden behind. As my intellect refines and tunes into the subtle, it keeps me free from illusion. Today let me refine my intellect and discern subtle truths.

14

We discovered the laws of physics, we did not create them. They exist whether we like them or not. Gravity will drop something on my head even if I don't believe in it. In the same way spiritual laws exist whether I believe in them or not. The law of reciprocity, of karma, ensures that I will get back what I give, whether I like it or not. Therefore, if I want to get I must first give. Today let me enjoy working with the invisible spiritual laws and give, knowing I will receive the fruit at a future point.

15

If my compassion does not include myself it is incomplete. If I do not give genuine compassion and kindness to myself it will be difficult for me to offer it to others. When I take care of myself spiritually, I am filled with compassion. This energy naturally extends outwards to others. Today let me express compassion for myself.

16

The sun's light creates a shadow when blocked. In the same way, a shadow in me is caused by something blocking my inner light. Shadows in the soul are created by buried traumas or negative experiences. I may not be aware of how this darkness influences me or dictates my reactions. In order to see it clearly I must face the shadow. Only then can I be free from its control. Today let me face the shadow to shed light on it and free myself from its invisible control.

17

When I do everything on time, life responds to me in a timely manner. When I value time I use it in a worthwhile way. When I value time, time values me. The karmic return of valuing something is to have it in abundance. Then unexpectedly things happen for me in a timely manner. Today let me use time well and enjoy the return.

18

Technology draws me into a world of unending, detail complexity and speed. When I know who I am, I am able to interact with technology without losing myself. Reflective moments alone in nature, or in a quiet corner at home, give me the chance to separate from technology and remember who I am. I am the one who USES the technology. I am the one who observes the impact of speed on my thinking process. I am also the one who can slow down at will and be still. Today let me remember who I am.

19

The act of de-cluttering shifts my focus from greed to need. When I learn the spiritual art of de-cluttering, I recognize the great value of accumulating subtle spiritual experiences. These fill my inner world with abundance and I lose the desire to accumulate physical possessions. Today let me experience living abundantly from the inside out.

20

It is said that 'empty vessels make the most noise'. Spiritual practice is the art of filling my mind with simple, clean and pure thoughts. I pay attention to this practice so the mind does not remain empty. Void and emptiness of the mind is not what I am looking for in life. I am looking for the full potential that comes from my innate virtues. Today let me fill my mind with the beauty of my qualities and potential.

21

An umbrellas protects me from getting wet in the rain. It doesn't stop the rain from falling. In the same way, my karma protects me. I will get back what I have given. If I have taken care of others, if I have done my best, I will get the return. It doesn't mean that rain won't fall and that it may even touch my head, but it does mean that I will feel protected. Protection comes in the form of inner power, tolerance, determination and support from others. Today let me protect myself by creating an umbrella of good karma.

22

Chasing after a desire is like chasing after a mirage. It is impossible to catch a desire. When I have a desire, it owns me and I am compelled to run after it. Even if I touch it for a moment and feel temporarily fulfilled, it will quickly disappear. Then my life becomes a chase. When I allow myself to be quiet and still for a few moments, I discover I have what I need already. When I experience being content I can stop chasing mirages. Today let me be still long enough to discover and appreciate the deep fulfilment within.

23

Every piece is needed to complete a puzzle. In the jigsaw puzzle of life, I am responsible only for my own piece. Other pieces surround me, but I must pay attention to myself. Do I show up peacefully? Do I discern what is needed and offer the best energy I can in each situation? Sometimes a situation requires silent acceptance, other times active input is required. Today let me take care of my piece of the puzzle.

24

I receive blessings from the hearts of others when I do something that benefits them. Blessings are experienced as unseen energy that uplifts me, helping me stay light. The greatest blessing is when my actions make someone else feel secure in their own capacity and strength. Today let me give happiness to others and experience the lift of blessings.

25

The intellect becomes blunt when over-focused on the material or sensate. When I become material-minded, I relate only to the concrete aspects of a situation. With the five senses as my only guides to what is 'real', I miss the subtle dimensions. A world of subtlety opens to me when I can detect nuance. Today let me explore the richness of nuance.

26

Good wishes sent to friends in need are experienced as a wave of good energy. If my good wishes carry worry with them, this will be felt by my friends as well. Then the energy I am sending is mixed. In order for my good wishes to have a positive impact they must be free from worry. When I calm myself I can fill my good wishes with pure, positive energy. Then they will bring benefit to others. Today let me ensure my good wishes are worry-free.

27

Never be defeated by defeatism. The ultimate defeat is to give up hope. When it becomes too frightening to be hopeful, even the smallest thread of hope can keep someone going. Hope appears suddenly when I stay open to its presence. Hope is experienced as a flush of positive energy guiding me to find new solutions. Hope keeps me ever-ready to try again. Today let me defeat defeatism with hope.

28

Happiness is an indicator of the well-being of a person and a society. Happiness is the basis of a healthy economy and a healthy person. When I am happy, I feel generous and I contribute more. When I am unhappy, I withdraw or take. Happiness is generated through giving to others. Today let me live with the awareness that happiness is the generous core of my existence.

29

Reactions waste precious energy and create difficulties in my relationships. However, my reactions also reveal information about myself and the situation. When I am able to detach from my reaction momentarily, I can interpret the data they convey. With the practice of being a detached observer, I can see the reasons why I am reacting. This can lead me to find new solutions. Today let me detach from my reactions and use the data they convey to find wise responses.

30

When I silence the chattering of the mind, I can hear what is in my heart. My heart is the keeper of the still purity that lies within the soul. My heart longs for silence because it contains the power to create harmony in all my relationships. It is a mirror to my own beauty and gives me the sweetness to sustain myself and others. Today let me sit quietly with my heart and enter the sweet realm of silence.

JULY

1

Raise your words, not your voice. It is rain that grows flowers, not thunder. Gentleness opens hearts more than anger will. A heart must be opened for the mind to consider something new. Today let me speak gently and open hearts to newness.

2

"Respect for another means offering advice only where there is the strength to accept it." Dadi Janki

It is a big responsibility to offer advice. Although it may seem helpful to offer advice, it is sometimes best just to listen. When a person is able to talk through their situation and their feelings with someone who listens, they discover for themselves what they need to do. Today let me support others to find their own way forward without giving advice.

3

What is on my mind can be seen through my eyes and actions. I may believe my thoughts are private but they reveal themselves in everything I do, especially the expression on my face. When I am aware that my thoughts are reflected on my face, I will ensure they are worth seeing. Today let me think well.

4

Generosity means more than just giving. The greatest act of generosity is to see beyond the weaknesses of another person. A generous heart will see the best in others. When I see past a weakness, I offer a mirror for someone to see their innate value. This requires a generosity of spirit, a big heart. Today let me use my generous heart to guide my eyes to see the strengths of others.

5

If it hurts, it's ego. Ego is a false image I hold of myself. If I am easily hurt, it is because an ego is being attacked. When this image is threatened, I experience an ego "death" and it hurts. Spiritually, my aim is to be free from ego. Thus, I am willing to hasten the process of ego death. An excruciating ego death is less painful than living under ego's rule. Just as a wound may hurt when it is cleansed, knowing it is the first step of a healing process allows me to tolerate the pain. Today let me free myself from ego.

6

When I reflect on how I got to where I am today, it is because of the choices I made in the past. My past has created my present. By choosing one path, I eliminated many others. Each choice opened new options for me. Today, I am exactly where I chose to be, so let me respect and accept full responsibility for the power of my choices.

7

At one time, dial-up broadband internet seemed fast. Now, it seems slow. What changed? The speed of my thoughts increased. Now, movies, the internet and other things from the past seem slow. When my thoughts move fast, my body follows. Then I expect things to happen quickly. This constant need for quickness makes me impatient and restless. Slowing down momentarily, I can regain perspective about what is most important to me; peace, happiness and love. Today let me slow down my thoughts.

8

Calm creates calm. In the face of great turmoil it takes only one person to be an example of sensibility, decency and calm to influence many others. If I wish to be one who brings calm to others in challenging times, I must practice on a daily basis. Today let me remain easy and calm in the face of all situations and strengthen my ability to offer calm when needed.

9

Be clear on your intentions. My character is illuminated by the coherence that exists between what I say and what I do, consistently, day in and day out. To express my highest character I must check my intentions regularly and ensure that my actions are consistent with my highest intentions. This self-alignment heightens my accuracy and integrity. This practice is called spiritual effort. Today let me express my highest character in everything I do.

10

Pain and suffering are different. Pain is a signal that something is wrong; in my body, actions or thoughts. Suffering is my reaction to pain. We live in a world that wants to avoid pain through distraction or numbing. When I pay attention to pain's message, I begin to free myself from suffering. By discovering the root cause of my dis-ease, I reclaim a sense of self-mastery and control over myself and the pain. Today let me accept and understand the message that pain is sending and free myself from suffering.

11

To be impressed by others is to make myself less. When I compare myself with others I suppress my own natural qualities. Then I can become disheartened or depressed. To be inspired by someone's qualities is to awaken them in myself. Then I can appreciate others and awaken my own qualities at the same time. It is a fine but significant difference; to be inspired but not impressed. Today let me be inspired instead of impressed.

12

The consciousness of 'mine' acts like a hand that grabs onto things and people. When I think that someone is mine, my partner, my children, I live with the illusion that I own them. This makes me feel I have the right to clutch and control. Then I lose my freedom. Just as a bird clutches a branch for temporary support but is able to let go and fly at will, my spirit flies when I am able to let go of the consciousness of mine. I feel lighter and my relationships are easier. Today let me experience the freedom of letting go.

13

Rather than pleasing others, become pleasing. When I try to please others, I run after them in subtle ways looking for approval, feedback or affirmation. When I become pleasing to myself, I instantly become pleasing to others. What makes me pleasing to myself? I am pleased with myself when I act according to my highest standard. Today let me please myself by staying true to my own standards.

14

Lighthouses don't move around looking for boats to save, they just stand there shining brightly. In the same way, a soul is completely still inside a body that moves. The screen of my mind is still, even when thoughts move across it. The more powerful I become, the more still I can be. My mind and my awareness can concentrate and focus on stillness. Then I become a beacon of peace in a noisy, turbulent world. Today let me be still inside.

15

A tightrope artist maintains perfect balance high above the ground. The slightest imbalance results in a fall. It does not matter which side of the rope they fall from, it is still a fall. As I strive to balance myself in daily living, I walk a fine line between extremes. Even an extreme of something good can pull me off balance. There are no right or wrong sides to fall from, just the aim to stay balanced. Today let me walk the fine line of balance with ease and dignity.

16

To give regard to the opinions and ideas of others is to tie the gathering in the thread of unity. Unity is created by giving regard. When people feel respected, they feel accepted and safe. Respect is the thread that creates unity in a gathering and enables people to experience a sense of belonging. Today let me give regard to others and create unity.

17

Behind all creation is silence. Silence is the essential condition, the vital ingredient for the creative process. It is a power in its own right. The artist starts with a blank canvas of silence. The composer sprinkles notes between periods of silence. The very core of my being, out of which comes all my thoughts, is silence. Today let me stop, take a minute, and listen to the silence within.

18

The mind is able to interpret out-of-focus pictures because the imagination fills in the blanks. The imagination guides the mind to interpret what the eyes see. If hampered or clouded, the imagination will not see even what is most obvious. Depending on my attitude or belief, I invent additional bits to create a fuller picture of what I expect to see in a person or situation. My view of a situation is, therefore, a reflection of my biases and beliefs. The inner eye of the imagination must be clean and focused in order to 'see' the full picture, accurately. Today let me guide my imagination to 'see' clearly.

19

The stars pull the imagination beyond the physical world. They inspire me to think bigger, to aspire for something greater. When the imagination is free to soar beyond the gravity of the mundane, wonders become possible. Today let me elevate my mind to possibilities beyond the ordinary.

20

After spinning a web, a spider turns and swallows its silken creation, recouping the energy used to create it. Like a spider, I create webs of activity, relationships, interactions and connections. In my final moments I will face and 'swallow' my creation by making peace with my life. Rather than waiting for the final moments, I can make peace with my creation on a daily basis, ensuring that I can 'swallow' what I have done. This daily conscience-clearing allows me to create a clean web. Today let me enjoy the beauty of a clean creation.

21

When I commit to something with a pure intention, I become unshakeable. Life will test my commitment but if I stand firm, eventually the challenges will give up. Victory is based on determination. Today let me commit fully to something with determination and become unshakeable.

22

The greatest gift I can give another person is simply to include them. Although I have preferences for who I spend time with, I can include others in simple ways throughout the day. I can ask someone about their well-being, offer to bring something back from the coffee shop or simply share a nod or a smile. Inclusion has the power to awaken a sense of belonging and well-being in others. Today let me give the gift of inclusion.

23

Almost everything is made better with a cup of tea. Making tea is like a ritual. It takes time to boil the water, carefully rinse the pot and let the tea steep. This is part of the soothing quality of the experience. To set a clear intention to have a cup of tea and take the time to prepare it with care, has already set in motion a process of finding ways to make things better. Today let me make things better in soothing ways.

24

Keep the door shut to sorrow. Don't allow it to come in. When I know what causes me sorrow, I have a duty to protect myself from it. When I see sorrow coming I can make wise choices to step away and not engage. Like caller I.D., I can choose not to answer. I have a right and a duty to keep myself free from unwanted energies by making careful choices. Today let me protect myself from negative energies.

25

It is best not to stare too long at my weaknesses or they will consume me. I must face the weakness and discover the hole in the soul that created it. This hole needs filling. When I redirect my attention to the positive I feed my strengths. Rather than denying the weakness, I look at it, and choose to focus on my strengths instead. In this way I build my strengths and they eventually overcome my weaknesses. Today let me give full permission for my positive qualities to dominate.

26

When I am aware that peace in the world begins inside of me I make it a priority to remain peaceful. Of course, agitation will arise as will irritation and impatience. My response to these eruptions determines my state of mind. To choose peace each time its opposite arises, is to train my mind and heart in the direction of peace. Today let peace begin with me.

27

Somewhere inside, I remember a better version of myself. This is why I get upset when I act in lesser ways. It's frustrating to not be my best. But how do I know what my best is? I have a benchmark recorded in my memory that acts as a reminder of what I was and what I can be. The harsh voice of criticism may have come later from someone else, but the memory of my highest standard is recorded within me. Today let me honour my memory of greatness and seek to restore myself to my best.

28

When a person is disconnected from their value and uniqueness they try to be different by standing out in the crowd. Being 'different' is based on a comparison with others. Ego makes me compare myself to others and attempt to draw attention to myself by standing out as different. The spiritual journey of the soul is to discover and appreciate the qualities that make me, me. Today let me honour my uniqueness and release the ego of trying to be different.

29

The results of cooperation are never owned by one person. Cooperation leads to collective creation. When I offer my hand to work on a task with others, the results will be communal. The energy of cooperation provides the offer without owning the results. Today let me offer cooperation and enjoy the satisfaction of shared results.

30

Character is virtue-in-action. The quality of my character is built on a bedrock of virtue. Virtues are the positive qualities of the soul. Each quality is unique and distinct (courage, gentleness, humour, determination). Yet all virtues are sourced from the same positive energy reservoir of the spirit. When virtue guides my behaviour, my intentions are pure and bring benefit. Today let me build my character on virtue.

31

Meditation is the deep absorption in subtle experiences my senses cannot reach. It is to experience the innate spiritual qualities of the soul. Meditation begins by turning inwards. As my awareness becomes more subtle I can discern my invisible qualities of peace, love, contentment and freedom. This absorption in my own qualities brings them to life, filling them with energy. Today let me enjoy a moment of absorption in the invisible qualities of me.

AUGUST

1

Gentleness is a great power. Gentleness is sometimes seen as a lack of strength because it does not force or disturb. The true weakness is to become aggressive when frustrated or unfulfilled. It requires spiritual power to remain gentle in a world of injustice and violence. Today let me experience the strength of gentleness.

2

The world is clenched with anxiety. If I wait for the games to finish before experiencing peace, it is uncertain how long I will wait. In the meantime my efforts to improve the world will be influenced by fear and control. By releasing my anxiety now, I allow the world to breathe a sigh of relief and my contributions to solutions will be guided by peaceful energy. Today, let me release into peace even as the games continue.

3

Bodies age. As they become old, skin sags and wrinkles, organs tire and metabolism slows. However, the beauty of the soul is always visible behind the eyes. Although I know the body will age, I must remind myself that my true beauty is internal, in the soul. Today let me remember my true beauty lies within.

4

Every experience leaves an imprint on the soul, like a memory recorded in my subconscious. These are like recordings on a CD and they shape my perception and understanding of the world. I must be careful what I record as it will replay at some point. There are times when I must delete a track so it won't play again and again in the future. At the end of each day I can check what has been recorded in my memory track, keep what I want and delete the rest. Today let me choose the tracks I wish to record in me.

5

Being decisive requires quick judgment to discern if something is right for me. Judgment offers clarity for action. However, when the capacity to discern is skewed, tainted or warped in any way by negativity, it becomes judgmental. Then, what was once a beautiful gift for clarity and action becomes a tool to hurt myself and others. Today let me use my judgment capacity to discern and decide.

6

There are so many uncomfortable things to face in this world, it is sometimes easier to turn away and not see them. When I turn and face a hard situation I am no longer running away from it in fear. Instead I am opening myself up to the possibility of understanding it. In doing so, I create a space in my heart and mind for compassion, mercy and love. Then love, not anger, fear or despair, will guide my search for solutions. Today let me face uncomfortable situations with love.

7

The tortoise beat the hare for a reason. Little changes and consistent effort over a long stretch of time have a great impact. Although fast changes may be satisfying, it is only in the consistent efforts made over a long period of time, that lasting change 'sticks'. Today let me honour the consistent effort I am making, no matter how small.

8

The subtle undercurrent of 'want' steals my peace. To be peaceful is to be free from expectations and to want nothing from anyone. When I release expectations I can experience peace. Today let me release expectations, accept what is happening and be peaceful.

9

I come into this world alone and I will leave alone. On my journey through life, many others stand with me, our stories overlapping. Like trees growing in the forest, my life is shaped by other parts of the ecosystem. If I am to grow tall and strong I must recognize the value of the diversity around me. In a diverse forest the growth of one element supports the growth of all. The journey of life flourishes most beautifully when I have good company. Today let me stand and maintain my integrity while also enjoying the companionship of others.

10

There is a physical source of light for the earth, the sun. There is no source of darkness in the universe. There is nothing physical causing darkness to exist, only the absence of the sun. In the same way, when I am in the 'dark' of negative energy, doubt, worry or fear, I am unable to see the light. It does not mean there is no light, only that I cannot see it. I return to light by becoming silent and reconnecting to the silent light of my inner being. Darkness is my loss of connection to this inner light. Today let me conquer darkness by remembering the light within.

11

I feel most alive when I am expressing my unique inner qualities. When I express my true self I add positive energy to the world. What lights me up? What makes my head and heart fill with such energy that I feel electrified, spiritually intoxicated? Today let me discover and nourish what lights me up.

12

When time is my master, I become a slave and rush in everything I do. When rushing there is no mental clarity, only compulsion. Paradoxically, the slower I move, with mental alertness, the faster things get done. And they get done well, reducing the time spent correcting mistakes or re-doing work. Mental lightness enables things to be done quickly. Today let me experience moving with the speed of light-ness.

13

When a tall ship comes into the harbour a modern city is dwarfed by the elegance and grandeur of the old vessel. It sits like a jewel of the past and people flock to see it, to be reminded of a grand time. In spite of the developments in technology, infrastructure and science, we are pulled by the civility, order and manners of old times. Manners and civility are attractive and never go out of style. Today let me bring a character of civility and manners to a modern world.

14

When was the last time you did nothing and just sat and looked out at the sky or up at the ceiling? When my value is defined by doing I need to do more and more to feel valuable. Sitting quietly to reflect helps me define myself in ways other than accomplishments. Behind the achievements and the to-do lists is the one who does ~ me. Separating the 'doing' from the 'doer' happens more easily when I stop for a few moments and remember who I am. Today let me put myself on a diet from doing.

15

An investment of time and energy is required for peace to be created in the world. When I invest my attention and my energy in something, it grows. When I value peace, I will invest my energy in positive thoughts to create peace. Today let me invest positive energy in the direction of peace.

16

Feelings and thoughts have their roots in past experiences. Frightening things have happened to each of us. When frightening events happen in the world, these old fears are activated in the me. They burst into the screening room of my mind, overriding self-control. I have also experienced compassion, love and safety. Throughout the day, when I see living examples of these qualities they feed the compassion that dwells eternally in my heart. Today let me activate my positive qualities to face and conquer fear.

17

How do I know what I am capable of until I try? Until I get myself 'to the table' of new situations I do not know my capabilities. Once at the table I may find I don't fit. Or I may find I bring a unique, unexpected contribution that is highly valued. Today let me step up to new experiences and discover more about myself.

18

At the core of my being is a pure, perfect, beautiful self, untouched by the less-than-perfect world around me. Having forgotten this core, I believe that I must try to improve or perfect myself. This thinking binds me in negative self-talk and can lead to perfectionism supported by the false belief that I can criticize myself into perfection. In reality, spiritual effort is the sweet and simple act of remembering and experiencing who I am at my pure core. When I hold this awareness of myself it becomes my reality and guides my perceptions, choices and actions. Today let me remember who I am.

19

Happiness is never then, it is always now. If I make my happiness dependent on achievement or outcomes I will always delay it to a future time. It is good to have aims and goals but not to make my happiness dependent on their achievement. Today let me be happy now.

20

The state of the world is a direct expression of humanity's state of consciousness. When human beings move faster, time speeds up. When our consumption increases we deplete more of our planet's resources. When I am aware of the direct relationship between my own consciousness and the state of the world, I see the importance of small personal efforts to change. When I uplift my consciousness I bring simplicity, generosity, peace and humility to the world. As I change the world changes. Today let me maintain a focus on my spiritual efforts to build a new consciousness and a new world.

21

The greatest indicator of spirituality is a graceful ease with others. Knowing myself well and being content with myself, allows me to be content around others, creating natural rhythms of harmony. Today let me express true spirituality by being graceful with others.

22

Everything starts with the heart. When the heart is honest and clean, the mind is clear. Sometimes memories of the past cloud my heart. With courage and a choice to bring closure to things of the past, I can heal. As I move away from the past and any sorrow carried from that time, it begins to fade. When I am free from the past I can be fully present. Today let me choose to clean my heart.

23

Tension in relationships is caused when I tie a thread or string of ownership to another person. This causes expectations as I try to control the other for fulfilment of my needs. This is known as spiritual bondage, an energetic knot that causes tension for myself and the other. To be free from bondage I must let go of the thread of ownership, the consciousness of 'mine'. Today let me fly free from the bondage of 'mine' and create relationships of love and respect.

24

When I fill my mind with the light of love, peace and happiness I transform it into a sacred space, free from sorrow. Then my very being serves. What I AM is what I give the world. This is true service. I don't DO service. I AM a server. Others around me can pick up positive vibrations to uplift them. Today let me honour the value of filling my mind with positive energy and radiate it to the world.

25

There are only eight notes in the musical scale. Music is made when you know how to put them in order. In life there are a few simple principles that relate in all situations; respect, kindness, love, honesty and peace. When I put these in the order best suited to each situation my life becomes music. To move to the music of virtues is to have a noble life. Today let me put the musical notes of virtue in the right order for each situation.

26

People are better able to hear what I have to say when they know I care. There is so much knowledge and so many opinions in the world that people have grown tired of listening. When people trust that I care they are willing to listen. Today let me convey genuine care before sharing my thoughts and opinions.

27

Honest realization brings transformation. When I realize something very deeply, it immediately changes me. A realization is a discovery about myself or about the nature of my reality. Transformation is the practical application of realization. If there is no change; there was no realization. Today let me bring realizations into reality and experience transformation.

28

Seeking praise is like eating unripe fruit; I experience temporary satisfaction, then a stomach ache. Just as a sugar high causes a low, feeding ego with praise makes me feel down afterwards. Self-respect is created by a quiet appreciation of honest effort and pure intentions. It is knowing my value without needing to boast, brag or be praised. Anytime I feed ego, I feel bad afterwards. Today let me feed my self-respect.

29

Dancers have such mastery of the body that they can leap and land with precision. They can also hold a posture of beauty and stability with grace, inviting the audience to feel strong and elegant just by watching. This is why the arts give so much meaning to our lives, they stimulate our highest qualities and make us dance in our minds as we watch. When I master my mind I am able to hold a posture of elegance and stability throughout the day. Today let me hold a graceful posture in my mind and dance with life.

30

The natural state of the soul is fullness. The experience of emptiness is unnatural and creates discomfort. The discomfort of emptiness drives me to seek fulfillment through experiences, books, objects or relationships. Paradoxically, the constant gobbling of new input numbs me to my emptiness but does not awaken my fullness. Taking moments to find the peace within allows me to experience fullness and awakens a memory of my natural state. Today let me experience natural fullness.

31

A weakness, by definition, has no strength. When I focus on a weakness I feed it with the energy of my attention and give it power. I feed anything I pay attention to. When I understand this principle I will choose what I feed. Today let me direct my attention towards strength and the positive situations I want to grow.

SEPTEMBER

1

Vibrations are like sound waves, invisible radiating energy. No obstacle, hurdle or mountain can stop them. Every thought has a vibrational frequency that affects the world around me in some way. Today let me radiate powerful thoughts.

2

Many spiritual and religious traditions have the practice of offering; flowers to the river, food to God. The greatest offering is to give my life to a cause or my heart to a commitment. The attitude of 'offering' is considered sacred because it integrates the spiritual qualities of humility and deep respect. When I find something I value and cherish, I will be willing to offer myself. Today let me *offer* myself with respect and humility to something I honour deeply.

3

Every small act of courage is a huge step towards the unlimited. My perception of my capacity and my potential is limited when I focus on what I have known or been in the past. Each time I do something new, especially when frightening or slightly beyond my comfort zone, I stretch my capacity AND my perception of what is possible for me. Today let me take little steps into the unlimited.

4

Love creates cooperation. Where there is love, people are ready to give their time, energy and wealth. When I have pure and positive thoughts for others it makes them loving towards me. Love enables all types of cooperation. Today let me fill myself with pure and positive thoughts for others and create a loving, cooperative environment.

5

A rose is fragrant whether it is in a garden or a garbage heap. The surroundings do not change the inherent nature of the rose. Do I allow my surroundings to change my fragrance? Fragrance is the energy that emanates from me, created by my attitude. I keep my attitude clean by using the art of reframing to generate positive thoughts, even in negative situations. My deep faith that there is benefit to be found in everything, allows me to hold this positive energy and keep my attitude fresh. Today let me remain fragrant in all surroundings.

6

It is impossible to change another person. I may inspire or encourage them. I might even browbeat them, but ultimately the desire to change must come from within them. In most cases, people feel their own weaknesses. Even if they cannot see them clearly, they know there is something wrong. Strength and courage enable someone to face what must be changed. When browbeaten, a person hides behind denial and justifications. Change needs the support of inner courage, fed with love and encouragement. Today let me support change with love, acceptance and encouragement.

7

It is not the distance but the first step that matters. I plan big projects, including my own spiritual development. Soon I discover that, no matter how big my vision, it is the daily commitment to small consistent steps that makes the greatest difference to success. Today let me be consistent in taking small steps forward.

8

I carry my deepest wounds locked in my subconscious. Memories and subtle impressions come from unfinished business, rooted in the past. The pain from these wounds comes to revisit, to block and paralyze me when least expected. Healing does not mean finding and treating each inner wound. It means going even deeper, past the wounds, beyond the distant memories and unfinished business to the core of myself, to the heart of my spirit. Here I find the light and warmth of my pure self. Today let me heal by empowering my original, eternal spiritual self.

9

Selfishness shrinks my world to the dimensions I consider safe. The illusion of safety becomes a comfort zone I then protect and defend. My true safety lies in living according to the law of karma. When I give with pure intention, I will receive. Today let me build true security by giving.

10

Beautiful thoughts create a beautiful world. Every action and thought has an impact on me and my surroundings. When I keep beautiful thoughts in my mind, my face softens, lightens up and becomes a portrait of beauty. Today's beauty contributes to a world of beauty tomorrow. Today let me hold beautiful thoughts in my mind so my face can be a beautiful portrait of tomorrow.

11

Behind the external, physical appearance and beneath the noise of thoughts and emotions in the mind, rings the silent note of the soul. My vibration is like an energetic frequency. It is my unique note. Every soul has a unique vibration or note. I discover my note by sitting in silence. This is my home-base. Throughout the day I can reset my vibration to this original frequency and feel like myself again. Today let me experience the vibration of my unique note.

12

Body and soul operate according to separate laws. The body is ruled by the material laws of physiology and biology. The soul operates according to the laws of energy. Consequently, the healing process will be different for each. Because the energy of the soul keeps the body alive it has a significant influence on the health of the body. Healing the soul is based on wisdom, love, peace and faith. To heal the soul I must take the medicine of virtues every day, morning and evening. This allows me to start my day with peace, love, gratitude and end my day with the same. Today let me heal the soul.

13

Non-violence is a very deep philosophy. It requires me to do NO harm physically, but also to avoid harming someone's self-respect. Such an ethic requires tremendous awareness and sensitivity. When I have learned to be gentle with myself, I can be the same with others. Today let me be completely non-violent.

14

My thoughts create my experience of reality. Even when people thought the world was flat, it was still round. They did not venture far from home, afraid they might fall off the edge. In the same way I have thoughts that are not true but still affect my experience of reality, limiting me in some way. Today let me consider my unlimited potential by freeing myself from limited thoughts.

15

The vessel metaphor of 'filling' myself with goodness implies I am empty and can be filled. In reality I am already full of goodness. I am rooted in goodness. My innate nature is good. I may not always feel connected to my goodness, but it is always there under the surface. I reclaim it when I remember it is there. Little by little, goodness becomes my primary identity and I feel filled. Today let me experience my innate goodness.

16

Waste thoughts are like typhoons in my mind. They create chaos, confusion and instability. As a result, I lose energy, time and confidence. It requires determination to put an end to waste thinking. Each time a waste thought arises I pack it up, like snapping a suitcase shut, and redirect my thinking to a more positive focus. When I reduce the waste in my mind, I am able to stabilize myself and focus forward on solutions. Today let me pack up waste thoughts.

17

When I am quiet, I become a silent witness to my inner truth. I know what is right for me and this clarity enables me to make decisions with confidence. Sitting still is a powerful tool for wise living. It doesn't take long, but it must be practiced regularly to experience the benefit of insight. Today let me create a habit of sitting still in silence to see what is real for me.

18

The industrious bee draws nourishment from plants and flowers, accumulating pollen that it carries from flower to flower as it travels. This tireless cross-pollinating fertilizes plants that would otherwise not reach each other. Without these sweet net-workers many plants would die. Like the bee, I travel through life taking wisdom from place to place while also contributing my qualities. The richness I gather is nourishing and serves to pollinate my growth and development. Like the bee I cross-pollinate ideas, activities and relationships to create a more beautiful world. Today let me enjoy cross-pollinating.

19

Only love can dissolve ego. When I encounter ego in someone my own ego is activated. To respond with ego is to enflame the situation. If I can find a way to soften my response, ego will dissolve. Today let me dissolve ego with love.

20

Northern peoples have many words for snow, each depicting a subtle aspect of its texture, weight, colour and density. This vocabulary is important because snow is a primary focus, affecting every aspect of life. I learn the words for subjects that interest me. On the spiritual journey, I discover an entirely new vocabulary of words to describe the subtle aspects of my inner world. Although the words for virtues may be known to me, I soon discover behind the word is a richness of subtle and nuanced experiences. Today let me explore a spiritual vocabulary.

21

No matter how much you try to hide the sparkle of a jewel, it cannot remain hidden. A jewel will sparkle even in mud. It will shine like a light that is seen in the dark. When I sparkle, I offer light to others. Even in a dark or murky situation when I keep myself lit from inside, others see the spark and draw comfort, inspiration or light. Today let me sparkle.

22

The human soul expresses its beauty through the physical body. The beauty of the physical face, even when aged, depends on the quality of the artwork inside. Inner artwork is called character. When my character is beautiful, then no matter how old the exterior, there will always be grace and dignity visible on the surface. Today let me honour and refine the inner artwork of my character.

23

Ego makes me inflate and deflate my sense of self. Sometimes I feel great about myself and other times, not. Ego has two faces. One face makes me think I am better than others, superior in some way. The other face of ego makes me feel small or less than others. Ego feeds on comparison, diverting my attention away from my intrinsic value as a human being with unique strengths and weaknesses. Today let me 'right-size' my sense of self by honouring my unique, essential nature.

24

A tree's personality is shaped over time by its internal and external environment. The seed has within it the DNA that determines what it will become. The conditions of the soil, water, air and human interaction will also mold and shape its growth. In the same way I am shaped by my external conditions. However, the seed of me is my spiritual DNA or blueprint, containing the gifts and qualities unique to me. Today let me discern the difference between my fundamental nature and the conditions that shape me.

25

Each day is filled with a hundred choices and decisions. Wisdom is my best guide. Wisdom comes from three places; experience, learning and intuition. Experience comes from engaging with life, learning from reflecting, and intuition from listening to my inner voice. Today let me listen to myself and discover the depths of my own wisdom.

26

Kings of old had their food checked to ensure it was free from poison. Thoughts are food for the soul. Each thought affects my mood and ultimately my body. Do I check my thoughts before I 'eat' or absorb them? By checking my thoughts, I can nourish myself (the soul) and remain healthy and powerful. Today let me check my thoughts and keep only the most nourishing ones.

27

If I see life as a battle I will struggle. If I see life as game I can enjoy playing. The video game sector thrives by transforming battles into games. Life provides me a series of obstacles designed to build my strength to advance to the next skill level. When I am involved in petty skirmishes or even big wars, I can become exhausted or I can develop stamina, depending on my approach. Today let me transform battles into a game and enjoy developing strength.

28

Sometimes it is hard to know how much effort to put into a situation or relationship. Sometimes I invest too much, other times I don't invest enough. It is part of life's maturing process to discover the right balance, the optimal investment for each situation. Optimal means 'just the right amount', neither too much nor too little. I can discern what is optimal by checking my conscience. It will pull at me if I am doing too little, and it will pinch if I am doing too much. Today let me discover optimal.

29

Flowers stretch towards the light in order to grow. The sun touches their petals and they open in response. The soul needs to experience the light of love and meaning in order to grow. I feel wealthy beyond measure when my life is full of meaning. Then I need very little from the physical world to live well. Today let me turn towards the light of a life filled with meaning and simplicity.

30

A diamond's flaw is part of its structure and must be removed with extensive rubbing and scrubbing. My flaws are the same. Beliefs and habits that have formed over time are so deeply etched into my self-image and worldview that I cannot even see them. They are only revealed to me when people or life situations rub me the wrong way. Although experienced as irritants, this rubbing is required to remove the flaw. Today let me accept and appreciate the rubbing aspects of life's purification process.

OCTOBER

1

Thoughts are like people, they are attracted to others like them. Thoughts are vibrations that create energy ripples through the body and through the room. Vibrations seek resonance. I will attract the same vibrations I emit. Today let me attract good company by emitting the vibrations I most wish to attract.

2

Over-thinking is the biggest disease of the mind, especially thinking about others. Thinking too much is like eating too much, it makes my mind heavy. It is impossible to suppress thinking but I can redirect my thoughts to a more positive focus. I experience high-quality nourishment when I am absorbed in a high-quality thought. Today let me go on a thought diet and consume only healthy thoughts.

3

I have no authority to forgive another person. Their actions, their conscience will come back to them. I can, however, forgive myself. To forgive myself means to face and acknowledge the ways I allowed myself to be deceived, dependent, needy and take sorrow. When I forgive myself, my feelings towards the other person change. True forgiveness means that my feelings change and I am able to give genuine good wishes to the other person. Today let me forgive myself.

4

Hiking, holidays and other 'get a-ways' provide an opportunity to get perspective on my life. I see and appreciate the beauty of my life more clearly when I am away than when I am too close. I also see where I need to make adjustments. Meditation is an opportunity to get away from my situation. Without leaving home or climbing a mountain, I can sit quietly, comfortably and allow my consciousness to soar above my life. With perspective I can see clearly, appreciate the best of what I have and make adjustments as needed. Today let me get perspective.

5

If, at any time, I lose hope in myself, I can simply look inside my heart and remember the good actions I have performed in my life. From the smallest to the grandest action, the happiness I have given to others reminds me of the purpose of my life and inspires hope. Today let me find hope in my heart.

6

In order to create good relationships I must use my mind to think about what I can learn from others. I must use my eyes to see their good qualities. I must use my words to recognize, value and appreciate their accomplishments. And I must use my actions to cooperate with others. Today let me create good relationships.

7

As I gather spiritual knowledge, life provides opportunities to test its relevance and validity. To know something without experiencing it, is NOT to know. As I deepen my reflective practice I can trust life to provide the practical test papers for me to apply my new spiritual discoveries. Each test requires me to respond with an elevated and accurate action, realize why the test occurred and recognize what needs to shift in order to be ready for a similar test in the future. Each test strengthens my capacity to respond. Today let me pass life's practical tests.

8

Every action has an equal and opposite reaction. Whatever I do, I do FOR or TO myself. Every action is like a seed that, when sown, produces fruit. The harvest will be good or bad according to quality of the seed of action. Today let me think before I perform actions and ensure I am sowing strong, positive seeds to reap beautiful fruit.

9

My experience of stress is a direct result of the pressure I am under and my level of resilience. When I build my resilience, I am able to mitigate the stress I experience, even in the face of increasing pressure. I increase my resilience when I make time daily to care for my physical health (exercise) and my mental health (meditation, prayer, reflection). Then, no matter how many hours I work, or how much pressure there is, my investment in my own resilience will reduce my stress. Today let me focus on increasing my resilience.

10

When I learn a sport I first learn the rules, then I develop the muscles, skills and stamina. Finally, I learn the subtle tactics of the game so I can see ways to conserve my energy and maximize the effectiveness of each action. In meditation I first develop the mental muscles and stamina to extend my patience beyond momentary distractibility. Then the subtle tactics become accessible to me. I see the bigger game of life and I understand how to conserve and maximize my energy. Today let me become skilled in the game of life.

11

We tend to see things not as they are, but as we are. What I see around me is painted by my mood. Becoming quiet inside allows me to check the lens through which I am seeing the world. Today let me check and change my inner lens.

12

We all have a third eye. We have two physical eyes to look at the world around us and one eye for looking inward. Why would we want to look 'in' when everything is happening 'out there'? Because the treasures of peace, happiness and love I seek are inside. Today let me take a moment to stop and use my third eye to look inwards and be aware of my treasures.

13

Worry is 'fantasized catastrophizing'. This is the act of creating a gruesome image of the future and using it to frighten myself. I can conquer worry by gently and lovingly coaxing my mind to create images of a positive future. My mind will try to return to the worry habit many times. Each time I must redirect it and engage my imagination to create positive scenarios. Today let me free myself from worry by using my mind to create positive images of the future.

14

When I firmly commit myself to something with a pure intention, I become unshakeable. A true commitment has determination within it. Without commitment, excuses will arise and distract me until I give up. Life will test my commitment but if I stand firm, eventually the challenges will give up. Victory is based on determination. Today let me commit with determination.

15

Love is not an emotion, it is my essential nature. In today's world love is considered an emotion. It is something that sweeps us away on a roller coaster ride of highs and lows. We have turned love into a commodity, something to be traded or bought and sold. When I experience my essential nature as love I no longer need to seek it outside. Love is my core energy and I can access it at will. Today let me be love-full.

16

The time of one who has an easy and light nature is never wasted. Work is work, it will eventually get done, but being spiritual is to be light as I do the work. What helps me be light? Lightness comes from the awareness that I am an actor playing a part in this wonderful drama of life. Each scene that comes in front of me tests my ability to maintain perspective and stay light. Today let me enjoy the drama of life and stay light.

17

Live simply so that others may simply live. This is a nice idea but most of us find our lives are more complicated and complex than ever. Simple means easy. Simple means asking, "is this really necessary?" Simple means keeping it short and sweet. Simple means keeping the focus of my attention on what I need to do now. Today let me find ways to simplify my life.

18

I am a human being not a human doing. Although I spend most of my time involved in activity, I am first and foremost a 'being'. Over-involvement in action has made me 'activity-conscious' and I define my value by what I do. Then I forget that being comes before doing. By making the effort to 'be' and hold the awareness of myself as a 'being' I bring greater power to everything I do. Then things get done more efficiently. Today let me 'be' first and then do.

19

It is easier to let go of something when I have a replacement. Until the replacement is available, I will keep the security of the 'old'. This is also true for old habits, even negative ones. Why would I let go of an old habit when it has been a companion for so long? When I invest in developing a new habit it is easier to let go of the old. The secret of transformation is to invest in something new. Today let me invest in new habits.

20

We can never really know someone fully. We cannot know who they have been or what they have experienced. When I look at the surface of a person I see only the details of their current expression. Surfaces can be deceiving and can distract me from seeing the hidden truth of a person. I must look deeper if I want to see the qualities and traits they have carried through time and recognize the depth of experience and wisdom stored within. Today let me see past the surface to the depth of each person.

21

Happiness is a product of peace. I cannot be happy if I do not have peace. True happiness comes from a feeling of contentment and satisfaction. When I am aware that I have everything I need inside I become peaceful. Meditation takes me inside to the contented core of myself where I have everything and need nothing. Today let me be happy and experience peace.

22

In the early morning hours the subconscious is unguarded and accessible to the conscious mind. This is the time for early morning meditation. When my subconscious is accessible I experience buried parts of myself, including the dark bits in the soul. To be alone with my inner world when it is so exposed (even raw) requires courage and a lot of love. This is a time of spiritual cleansing. To hold an intention to be fresh and functional during early morning meditation is heroic. If I can do this, I can do anything. Today let me enjoy an early morning meditation.

23

Indulgence feeds the ego not the soul. Any time I allow myself to indulge in anger, greed, desire or attachment I am starving the soul of its innate qualities of love, peace and bliss. When I feed the soul, ego is starved of my attention and its negative emotions subside. Today let me feed the soul.

24

Peace is more than the absence of conflict. Permanent peace comes from a change of thinking, a change of heart and the inner power to act from my highest state of mind. Even when I am fully committed to peace, when triggered, my reactions may not be peaceful. Spiritual knowledge purifies my thinking. Healing purifies my heart. When my attitude is peace, my commitment is peace and my heart is peaceful, there will be permanent peace. Today let me build peace from the inside out.

25

A green luscious garden does not catch fire as easily as a dry forest. Kept healthy, a garden can become a little oasis inside a ring of fire. I must nourish my inner garden so it doesn't become dry. I provide nourishment by feeding it the soil of positive thoughts, watering it with sweet solitude and pruning waste through honest reflection. Today let me nourish my inner garden and make it an oasis.

26

When I let others define me I lose myself. All day I am defined by what I do and who I am with. I am defined by my job, my profession, or lack thereof. I also take my sense of identity from the people I spend time with. My family and friends see me in a certain way and this shapes how I see myself. Today let me define myself by who I am at my core.

27

Newspapers, television and coffee shop conversations are filled with negative news and complaints. Multiple sources vie for my attention to deluge me with negativity and fear. I have the power to choose where to focus my attention, to train my mind to see beneath the surface and find goodness. Although knowing what is happening in the world is important, more important is my ability to offer positive energy to keep goodness alive. This protects me from negativity. Today let me keep goodness alive by training my mind to pay attention to the positive.

28

Thorns on a rose stem serve to protect the rose. In the same way the thorns of difficulties I encounter in life are often for my protection. Obstacles are instrumental to protect me from over-extending myself or getting trapped in ego. Difficulties bring me back to myself with humility and renew my commitment to simple spiritual effort making. Today let me appreciate the thorns that remind me to protect my inner beauty.

29

Patience teaches me not to push, but rather to wait. Patience also teaches me to observe and appreciate the natural rhythms of life. Everything happens in its own time, even if I wish to rush it. I understand that nothing remains the same, everything changes at some point. This understanding allows me to watch and wait. Today let me practice the art of patience.

30

What is my relationship with the future? Do I plan relentlessly in hope of controlling the outcome? Do I live in the future rather than the present, eagerly anticipating the next event? Or do I invest positive energy in each moment, knowing this will reap double return; happiness in the moment and a positive future? Today let me create a positive relationship with the future by investing in the present moment.

31

What are you paying attention to, the foreground or the background? In the foreground there is noise, action, and sometimes chaos. But in the background, there is silence. Silence is the background to everything, including the noise in my head. When I get absorbed in silence, I turn down the volume on the foreground and turn up the volume of peace in my mind. Today let me enjoy the background of silence.

NOVEMBER

1

Solutions are created when courage steps forward to face reality. When I have the courage to face what is in front of me I am able to find solutions. Beneath the noise and turmoil of the current times, the heartbeat of humanity is growing stronger. Today let me awaken to the possibility of solutions.

2

What does it mean that everything happens for a reason? Does it mean that life is teaching me a lesson or that bad things occur to punish me for previous wrongs? When I consider that every situation has benefit, then life becomes my friend rather than my character-reformer. Today let me see life as my friend and benefit from every situation, even hard ones.

3

Motivation is driven by a goal, for example 'to win the race'. Intention is much more subtle. It is based on deep feelings within the heart that become the driver behind my goals and aspirations. Motivations are more obvious but to see an intention requires a deeper look into the self. If I fail to win the race, does my drive dissipate; my hope and self-belief falter? Pure intentions give me the resilience to carry on. If my intention is pure, then win or lose, I will carry on with self-respect. Today let me check my intentions.

4

In a world of constant stimulus I develop the inability to tolerate boredom. I begin to seek more and more stimulation; for my ears, eyes, taste buds and body. Through meditation, I develop a rich inner life and I lose the need for external stimulation to feel satisfied or entertained. I learn to step inside myself, discover the treasures within and be content. Today let me explore my rich inner world.

5

The way I treat the people I strongly disagree with is a spiritual report card on what I have learned about love, compassion and kindness. I know I have attained a high level of spiritual maturity when I am able to treat a person I do not like or respect, with kindness. It is easy to be kind to people I like. It is much harder to maintain respect at all times, with all people, including those who oppose me. Today let me be kind...always.

6

True governance begins by learning to govern myself. I learn to govern myself by overcoming bad habits and negative actions. This enables me to participate in collective governance. When there is a shared understanding of the highest and best behaviour together with the inner power to enact it, there will be a common expression of true living. Today let me contribute to a positive form of governance by governing myself.

7

I weaken my heart when I take sorrow. To say someone has hurt me is evidence that I have taken sorrow. It is up to me whether or not I allow another person's words, attitude or actions to affect me. I need not allow them to touch my inner core. When I do, I become hurt. Today let me decide not to take sorrow.

8

A master chef gathers the freshest ingredients before cooking. This care extends to grinding and blending their own spices. Similarly, great care is needed in gathering and processing spiritual knowledge. I gain the most valuable insights when I delve deeply into the spiritual wisdom I am accumulating. This is known as 'grinding my own ingredients'. The effort I make to discern the meaning and relevance of knowledge to my life will nourish my spiritual growth. Today let me grind my own spiritual ingredients and nourish the soul with the best possible nutrition.

9

There is a big difference between being nice and being pure. Nice can be a thin coating over feelings of aggression or disregard. Pure is a deep experience of respect for myself and others. Purity generates deep kindness combined with the clarity and firmness. Today let me focus on purity.

10

Natural cycles exist in matters of history, economy, spiritual energy and human potential. At the start of a cycle I gather the energy, wealth and resources required for the new creation. Then I must hold and sustain the creation long enough for it to mature. After maturity I must let it go, I must give it away so it flows and serves others. If I hold on too long it will stagnate. If I let go too early, it will not survive. To master this process is to create abundance in my life. Today let me practice the art of creating, sustaining and letting go.

11

Infinity is a symbol that represents energy flowing from the past to the future and back again, through the point at the centre. Life's patterns repeat in a similar cycle. I can watch from the centre point, detached and still, as life's patterns flow in and around me. Today let me observe patterns from the centre of myself.

12

I live with the illusion of independence in a world of growing dependency. I depend on people I do not know to produce the food and materials I use on a daily basis. I cannot take care of my basic needs without many other people, even to get the simplest thing to my door (my morning cup of tea or coffee.) This creates an uncomfortable paradox called 'helpless independence'. In spite of my belief that I am independent, I am increasingly dependent. When I recognize my inter-dependence, I feel more connected to my global family. Today let me be aware of the subtle threads of connection and appreciate the inter-dependence that makes living possible.

13

A person who has discovered their true value will never diminish or exaggerate their worth with an illusory identity based on labels and external achievements. Today let me value myself.

14

As wisdom increases, the need for words reduces. Wisdom is found in silence. Behind the words, behind the feelings, behind the thoughts lies a place of deep quiet and calm. Here is where wisdom resides ~ in the still and silent core of my being. Wisdom sees through the noise and static to the truth in each situation. Today let me enjoy stepping back from words and visiting the quiet place of wisdom within.

15

Your perception of me is a reflection of you. My reaction to you is an awareness of me. I see everyone through a lens of my own experiences, shaping my view of myself and the world around me. This lens of the past transmits part of me onto everything I see. Although I may think I am seeing clearly without bias, everything I see is perceived through a personal lens. My purest lens is the foundation of my being ~ peace, love and respect. Today let me see everyone through a pure lens.

16

In a world where everything has become commoditized, I pay for everything from water to songs. When every human kindness becomes a monetized service, how do I foster generosity, without it becoming a business deal? How do I ensure that I am giving from the heart rather than strategically to get a return? Checking my intentions allows me to see where there is generosity and where there is selfishness. When I give from my heart, my spirit swells and I receive generosity in return. Today let me give freely.

17

Love, peace and happiness are my deepest values. They are also the deepest values of humanity. When I live my values I am happy, I feel a sense of integrity and wholeness, and I am protected from fear. As fear increases in the world around me, I must remain true to my values, both for myself and as a reminder for my human family. Today let me value peace and live my values.

18

Deep inside my consciousness is an oasis of peace. This is the molten core of the soul, but it is not hot, it is cool. When I draw energy from this cool oasis I am empowered to create peaceful thoughts and make accurate decisions. When I learn to live from this centre, peace becomes my companion, positivity my partner, and I am able to plant seeds of peace anywhere, anytime. Today let me visit the cool oasis of my core.

19

Every thought is filled with energy. Energy is like colour. I paint my mind with the colour of the energy I allow in my thoughts. Then I paint my world with these same colours. When I check my life, I can see where there are bright colours that I have painted with love, happiness and peace. There are also places that need brightening. Today let me fill my world with beautiful colours.

20

Frustration and anger are products of non-acceptance. There are so many things in this world that do not go as I would like. I need tolerance power to save myself from the constant inner pressure of anger and frustration. To tolerate is to accept that something is happening other than I would like. Although I may not agree, at least when I accept, I conserve my energy and create space to discover new ways to navigate the situation. Today let me change my response by developing tolerance power.

21

Self-control does not mean to suppress my emotions. Self-control is the ability to create my thoughts and feelings in spite of inner reactions. Today let me exercise self-control by creating the feelings I want.

22

An oasis is defined as a fertile spot in the desert, where water is found. It is a haven for weary travelers looking for relief. Life in our busy world can leave us feeling parched. Can I find the oasis within? That still place inside where I find rest and relief? Today let me sit in a silence oasis of peace and tranquility.

23

A beautiful dress can change the outer appearance but beautiful behaviour can change a life. Behaviour filled with virtues and manners is civilized. It is a result of having civil eyes ~ seeing the world through a spiritual lens. Civil eyes see others as souls and notice the subtle beauty and sparkle of each person. This creates a civilized world. Today let my behaviour be civilized by seeing the world through civil eyes.

24

To change the world we must change the systems that bind it. The existing systems are an expression of the human thinking that created them. Thinking must change in order for systems to change. Systems built to protect, can become oppressive over time. Changing consciousness means creating new thought-systems. When a critical mass of people create sustainable inner systems of respect, acceptance and peace, it will change the world culture and systems. Today let me change the world by changing my thoughts.

25

My life is my masterpiece. Its beauty depends on the choices I make. Each word spoken or written, each brush stroke of action will ultimately become part of my creation. Am I choosing the right words? Am I expressing the right, actions? Today let me make choices that add beauty to the masterpiece of my life.

26

No anger inside means no enemy outside. When I am at peace within myself I no longer seek fights, arguments or battles of any kind. I may still stand up for something, but I will do it quietly, peacefully with no anger inside. Discovering and expanding the peace inside frees me from enemies outside. Today let me enjoy a peaceful inner and outer world.

27

Just as the physical heart keeps the body alive by pumping fresh oxygenated blood to all parts, the spiritual heart keeps the soul alive with pure energy of love, peace, bliss. Those I love are in my heart because they remind me of my highest, best qualities. When God is in my heart I am reminded of the highest energy of the universe and rise to this highest level. Today let me fill my spiritual heart with the oxygen of pure energy.

28

Peace is not a passive attitude; it is an active state of mind. It requires constant attention to respond peacefully to life's upsets. The power of peace helps me let go of sorrow, worry and resentment. Activating peace, as a state of mind allows me to be free. Today let me awaken my inner power of peace.

29

Duality means two; two elements that are different such as two points of view or two ways. Polarity is created when I invest one element with positive energy and the other with negative energy. This creates energetic poles or opposing energies causing an inner push and pull between attraction and rejection, like and dislike, good and bad. In reality, without the value judgment and the injection of positive or negative energy, they are just two different things. Today let me discharge polarity by releasing judgment and appreciating differences.

30

You cannot control the speed of a river but you can control the speed of your boat. In white water canoeing the only time you are in control of the boat is when you go slower or faster than the river. To go the same speed as the river is to let the river control you. It is not sustainable to go faster than the river for more than a few moments, although a sudden surge of energy can get me past a rock or over a trough. Going slower is possible to sustain for a long time, back-paddling and hovering peacefully while the river rushes beneath the boat. Time can be compared to the river, it rushes by. I have no control over time, but I can control the speed of my movement. Most often, I try to outrun time, to go faster than time. This is unsustainable and causes exhaustion and dis-ease for body and mind. When I move slower than the current, I experience a sense of self-control. Today let me slow down and master myself in the currents rushing around me.

DECEMBER

1

Fewer words when thoughtfully chosen, have power. When I speak too much, my words lose power and people stop listening. There is power in my words when I concentrate on the essential. Silence enables me to attune myself to deeper aspects of a situation. Then I find words that bring benefit. Today let me speak fewer words of essence.

2

Imagine that each of us has a destination ~ a place or state of being. This destination is perfectly suited to who I am and a perfect expression of my potential. I spend my life moving towards this destination. Whenever I deviate from my route, the GPS recalculates and shows another way to get there. Even when the choices I make take me on a detour, ultimately life, like a GPS, brings me back on track to my destination; because it is mine. Today let me appreciate how life keeps bringing me back on track to myself.

3

The world rearranges itself around one who is stable. Like an obstacle in a river, or a stalled vehicle on a busy road, life moves around something that is fixed. When I stabilize myself, I become the centre point around which my life organizes. When I am in constant movement, I do not allow my life to adjust to me. Today let me be a still stable point and give my life a chance to organize around me.

4

BUSY is a form of laziness, a distraction from the real work of focusing on what matters most. Busy-ness can be a way to escape my inner world, an attempt to outrun my own thoughts. Sometimes being busy is an attempt to prove my value in physical achievements when I do not feel it internally. When I measure my value by how productive I am, I need to keep producing in order to feel valuable. Today let me be still for a moment and consider the role of 'busy-ness' in my life.

5

There are times when words do not help, when the only thing to do is to BE. At times, my peaceful, supportive presence is the most valuable offering I can make. There is great power in being a peaceful presence. When someone is unable or unwilling to hear my words, the energy of my presence can melt, soften and unlock a hard attitude or a broken hearts. Today let me be a presence of peace.

6

The habit of blame towards myself or others is an expression of anger. Anger is a secondary emotion. Hiding behind anger is hurt, sadness, fear or shame. When I discover the root of my anger, I can begin to heal. As part of the healing process, I take responsibility for my part in giving or taking past sorrow. This frees me from blame. I am responsible but not to blame. Today let me be responsible yet honour my blame-less self.

7

In temples and homes, idols sit on shelves above the activity of daily living. This place of honour is a sign of regard for the higher consciousness we ascribe to them. When I keep my consciousness high above I maintain a perspective that enables me to maintain my self-respect and respect for others. When I respect myself, I automatically receive respect from others. Today let me maintain an elevated attitude and give and receive respect.

8

The bounty of nature provides medicine to heal the human body. Plants and flowers, when knowledgeably combined, stimulate a healing response. Light and lovely or pungent and strong, nature's magic interacts with the biology of the body to support health. The food I eat becomes absorbed into my blood and cells, strengthening or weakening my body. In the same way, the food of thoughts either strengthens or weakens the mind. Today let me support healing with a healthy diet.

9

When I value something, I take care of it and I experience the fortune of having it. When I value my family, I take care of it. When I value my time, I use it well. When I value myself, I take the time to genuinely care for myself. When well cared for, I am able to care for every part of my life. Valuing myself is a great investment. Today let me value myself and bring value to others.

10

Self-respect is not a matter of WHAT I am doing in my life but HOW I am doing it. When I bring quality and virtue into each action, whatever that action may be, my self-respect grows. Today let me respect the HOW of what I do and grow my self-respect by bringing my best to everything.

11

Balance requires an understanding of the fulcrum, the point of maximum strength and stability. Being out of balance puts strain on my body and mind and topples the carefully constructed parts of my life. The fulcrum of human life is the soul. When I am too externally focused with little healthy attention to my inner world, my being experiences strain. To stay balanced in life, I must return to the centre-point of awareness. When I hold this fulcrum, I am at my strongest and can carry weight more easily. Today let me create exquisite balance by focusing on the fulcrum of the soul.

12

Soya sauce is made through a slow process of fermentation. Liquid sits outside in clay vessels, in heat and cold, for 2-3 years in order to ferment properly. Inside these plain containers is a vibrant life of pro-biotics, acting on the liquid over time to create a flavour we call soya sauce. As a soul, I live in a clay vessel, the human body. Inside this vessel, I have an active life of growth and transformation. I cannot always see what is happening inside as the vibrancy of the inner work is done in silent solitude. Today let me appreciate my spiritual maturing process.

13

The primary colours of the soul are peace, love, happiness, purity and power. When I search for these qualities through external means such as friends, food, entertainment or possessions, I become tired and often disappointed. To discover my own primary colors is to paint a sustainable life. Today let me use my primary colours to paint my life.

14

When I am caught in the maze of stressful thinking my response is to run this way and that, looking for a way out. By hurrying and scurrying, I create more confusion. It is best to stop and rise above the problem. A moment of detached perspective enables me to see the patterns and choose a clear path forward. Today let me move to higher ground and watch pathways reveal themselves.

15

If I cannot admit a mistake, it is because of ego and the fear of looking bad. A mistake unacknowledged, grows like a cancer in the soul and I begin to justify my actions. I then blame others, further distancing myself from self-accountability and mastery. It takes courage to face a mistake and admit it. It is easier to do this when I understand that the mistake itself does less harm than not admitting it. Today let me have the courage and humility to admit a mistake ~ even just to myself.

16

When dying fabric, dark cloth must be bleached to lighten it before another color can be added. It is the same with the soul. Where there is darkness in me, I must first be exposed to light to create a clear space for newness. When I am exposed to the light of pure energy ~ my own core qualities and the light of the Divine ~ I am coloured by these. Today let me wash away darkness with light and be coloured by virtues.

17

The energy of the soul is pure love. This energy is naturally expressed as generosity. I am generous by nature. I feel at my best when I use my time, energy and thoughts to generate benefit for myself or others. When I send my thought energy to the world around me with care and appreciation, I create a world of beauty and I am happy. Today let me express my natural instinct to give.

18

Many of us stare at computer screens for hours during the day without moving our bodies. Yet we find it difficult to sit still even for a few minutes in meditation. Why? When working on computers my intellect is actively engaged in some kind of creation. My mind is filled with the images of what I am creating (even spreadsheets). And my focused concentration gives me a feeling of power. For meditation to be equally engaging, I must use my intellect to think of something that interests me. I can create images to entertain the mind and generate a feeling of inner power through concentration. Today let me engage myself in meditation.

19

When my mind is happy, my consciousness expands. An expanded clear mind can discern the big picture and the small details of my situation. This enables me to make choices easily, without struggle. Today let me clear my mind and settle into a positive state before trying to discern pathways forward.

20

If an egg is broken by outside force, life ends. If broken from the inside, life begins. Great things come from inside. My potential acts like an inner force, pushing to express itself. Life circumstances support this by creating opportunities to grow. Today let me nurture my potential and express it externally.

21

When a vista beckons on the horizon, I move towards it. Although the destination may be clear, the path is not always visible and I must create my own. A path is not built all at once but with small steps laid down bit by bit until a path is created to reach my destination. A spiritual path is built with simple steps such as a daily meditation practice and the habit of redirecting my thoughts. These small steps build a pathway to my destination of spiritual development. Today let me build a path to my destination ~ bit by bit.

22

A good head and a good heart are a formidable combination. Imagine a heart that can forgive ~ even the worst of things. And a head that is sensible, practical and sees beyond polarities to find wise solutions. Today let me bring my good head and heart together, and bring compassionate wisdom to my life.

23

The soul resides behind the forehead in the frontal part of the brain. This central vantage point is like the control room in the human body. Here I can use my eyes to see, my ears to hear, my mouth to taste and my nose to smell. These sense organs take in information constantly throughout the day. But it is I, the thinking being, who interprets the data that enters. Although this process is invisible, the results are visible on my face, and in my actions and words. Today let me honour the private, silent world behind my eyes.

24

We are the underground. We are the seeds planted in the soil of this earth, covered by a bed of protective compost from the world's decay. Our roots stretch deep, anchored in the soil, providing stability for the new creation. When the sun warms us enough, we break through the soil and push upwards to the light. Deep within me is a seed of purity, a memory of innocence. This pure spirituality is growing, nurtured by the roots of values and virtues that connect humanity. We are the underground. Today let me nourish the roots of a new era for humanity.

25

Let there be peace on earth ~ and let it begin with me. There will be peace on earth when there is peace in the hearts and minds of human beings. When I make the effort to forgive, to let go, to offer generously ~ I contribute to peace on earth. Today let peace begin with me.

26

It takes courage and enthusiasm to leave the comfort of home, to spread my wings and fly. Enthusiasm comes when my motivation to leap is propelled from inside ~ when my part, my path, my potential call me to move. Today let me hear my potential calling and leap towards it.

27

The script of my life was written by the choices I made in the past. Each action determined a direction and guaranteed a return. I cannot change what I have done but I can write a new story for my future. This depends on the choices I make NOW. With careful consideration of what I would like the next chapter of my life to be, I can choose actions that will write the script for my future. Today let me write the next chapter with actions that create the story I want to live.

28

An attitude of gratitude fills the mind and heart with abundance. Gratitude is based on an awareness that I have received something. Even if I have not yet received it, I can be grateful in advance. This creates a feeling of inner abundance which invokes its own return. Today let me adopt an attitude of gratitude in advance.

29

When friends or loved ones experience difficulty, we want to help them find their way, we want to show them a path through the dark forest. We therefore offer solutions, opinions and advice. But what they really need is quiet loving energy that leads them to find their own path. This energy of hope and support acts like a gentle hand, pulling back the brambles to reveal a clearing filled with light. Today let me send loving energy to those in distress so they can find their way.

30

True self-respect is an attitude of inner dignity. It means being loyal to the royal within me. Behind my mistakes and the noise of my inner critic, exists a royal, dignified being. Today let me hold my head high with self-respect.

31

As the year ends, I reflect on the value of my efforts to stay true to myself and offer my best to the world. I honour the good fortune to be able to serve and assist others. And I appreciate myself and the love that keeps me reaching for my highest and best. As a new year dawns, I acknowledge the newness this past year has given me and I greet the newness to come. Happy New Year!

The Brahma Kumaris World Spiritual Organization (BKWSO) is an international NGO and a worldwide spiritual movement dedicated to personal transformation and world renewal.

Founded in India in 1937, it has meditation centres in over 110 countries on all continents, and is in consultative status with the United Nations.

Their aim is to help individuals transform their perspective from material to spiritual in support of the cultivation of a deep collective consciousness of peace and individual dignity of each soul.

Brahma Kumaris is the largest spiritual organisation in the world led by women. The founder, Prajapita Brahma Baba, put women in front from the very beginning.

All courses and programs are offered free of charge as a community service.

RAJA YOGA MEDITATION

Meditation is seldom associated with history or the concepts of time and space. It is seen, rather as a method to escape the details of such things.

Raja Yoga meditation recognizes that the natural thirst of the soul for truth and understanding, for meaning and significance, for purpose and identity must be satisfied before the "peace that surpasseth all understanding" can be achieved through the technique of meditation.

Raja Yoga Meditation, as taught by the Brahma Kumaris centres worldwide, consists of the topics below.

For more information contact a meditation centre near you:

www.brahmakumaris.org

Self-Realization

Raja Yoga is the practice of understanding and realizing the self as a soul, a being of consciousness, located in the centre of the forehead behind the eyes, in the brain (the software inside the hardware of the brain). As a tiny spark of spiritual light, eternal, imperishable, each of us is innately peaceful and loving. Letting go of the consciousness of the body identity results in self-realization and the powerful but subtle shift of consciousness from *"I am a body and I have a soul"* to *"I am a soul and I have a body."*

Yoga or Union with the Supreme Soul or Spiritual Parent

There is much confusion and controversy surrounding the existence and nature of God and God's role in the world. Exactly who is God? Does God really exist? Does it matter anyway? These are not just academic questions. They go right to the heart of the problems facing the world. Different religions have different ideas about who God is and how God should be worshipped. These differences have caused much conflict.

In Raja Yoga, it is understood that God is also a soul, with all the highest qualities of peace, love, bliss, clarity and power to a supreme degree. One can reach out to God with pure thoughts and experience the response of pure feelings and spiritual strength to begin to transform. Meditation is a way to re-create and strengthen a link with God.

The Philosophy and Law of Karma

"For every action there is an equal and opposite reaction." "As you sow so shall you reap." Both are expressions of an understanding of the immutable law of karma. Understanding this law sets us free from wondering, Why me? Why now? Why this? In the context of our relationships with others, karma explains everything. As eternal beings, we have written the current script of our lives with past actions and we are writing the future script of our lives with actions chosen now.

Spiritual Power

Through a body-conscious or physical lens, power is expressed as dominance (even subtle dominance of opinion or pressure). Force creates resistance, whereas spiritual power attracts. The current dynamics of force and resistance present in our world are a result of a lack of spiritual power. Spiritual power is the subtle energy that transforms situations, in benevolent ways. Meditation enhances the inner power to improve the qualities of one's response to life's challenges.

The Cycle of Time

Time can be seen as a cyclical process and therefore eternal. The earth and humanity move naturally from the "highest, most ordered state" to a more degraded, conflicted and fragmented state. This process happens slowly over time as a result of the loss of energy. Massive spiritual power is required to regenerate earth's potential, and this is done through human consciousness.

The Tree of Life

The story of human history and geography as told through the lens of the world's great religions. Each religion offers a timely message to uphold the core virtues and values of humanity, suited to the specific language and cultural context of the time and place. All branches of the tree originate from the same roots—the timeless values that hold humanity together—and the same seed, the Supreme Source. When these values are lacking, the world falls into conflict. A reconnection to the spiritual essence of each one's religion leads to regeneration.

The TIME is now

Human consciousness returns to its original state of peace, love and silence, letting go of the attachments, ego identities and desires that were generated in a materialist mindset. Love motivates all actions. The energy holding together the material world shifts, transforming old to new with the massive infusion of pure positive energy from the Supreme Power Source.

The cycle turns.

Made in the USA
San Bernardino, CA
26 January 2020